AMAZING AND EXTRAORDINARY FACTS

GHOSTS

GHOSTS

Malcolm Day

RP

RYDON
PUBLISHING

A Rydon Publishing Book
35 The Quadrant
Hassocks
West Sussex
BN6 8BP

www.rydonpublishing.co.uk
www.rydonpublishing.com

Revised edition first published by Rydon Publishing in 2018
First published by David & Charles in 2011

A CIP catalogue record for this book is available from the British Library.

ISBN: 978-1-910821-18-3

Printed in Poland by BZGraf. SA

CONTENTS

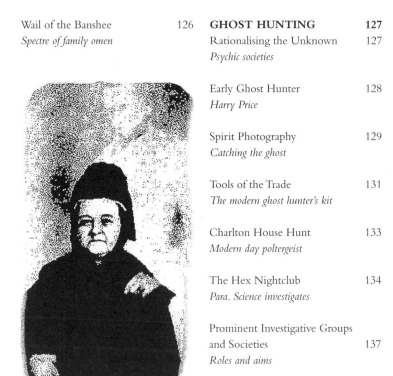

Salman Rushdie,
"What's a ghost? Unfinished business, is what."

The Satanic Verses

INTRODUCTION

Spook, ghost, wraith, phantom, spectre – what do they all mean? Are they all synonyms or is each one subtly different from the other? Is there a whole parallel universe out there made up of these entities? As Arthur C Clarke pointed out, there are 30 members of the dead for every person alive. That is heavy outnumbering.

Ever since the world began the human race has entertained ideas of the dead returning to haunt or guide the living. Every civilisation is said to have a belief in spirits. Countless examples can be found today among the indigenous cultures of North and South America, Asia, Africa, Australasia. In Western Europe societies have tended to 'outgrow' them, as adults will leave behind childish things on coming of age. Yet our ancient forebears in the classical traditions of Greece and Rome paid heed to ghostly machinations. Homer describes Hades as a place filled with shadowy ghouls that cry out beseeching the living for libations of freshly spilled blood. Battlefields were littered with spirits of the dead. Those who died a violent death, in any arena, might return for vengeance. In Virgil's *Aeneid*, those who ferry across the Styx in Charon's boat would see shoals of dead souls swarming about them.

Virgil's Aeneid

Delphi Oracle

From Seers and Oracles to Mediums and Séances

Foretelling the future was a special facility said to belong to privileged members of ancient societies. These seers would call up spirits of the dead using sacred forms of divination embedded in ritual. Prophets of the Old Testament in the Ancient Near East warned against this practice – necromancy – for it meddled in an unpredictable world of evil spirits. The witch of Endor conjured the spirit of Samuel, deceased king of Israel, at the request of Saul. So incensed was the former monarch at being disturbed that he refused to offer any advice to the new king. The 'witch' was probably no witch at all, but rather a kind of oracle similar to those in ancient Greece, such as Apollo at Delphi. Oracles would be consulted by mediums who would fall into a trance to obtain messages from the gods or the dead.

It is only a short step from this milieu of ancient fortune telling to the modern idea of a séance conducted by a medium believed to be empowered with the means to contact the dead. Mid-19th century America and Britain was gripped by such a vogue known as Spiritualism. Gatherings of the curious and the gullible, usually at the invitation of an eccentric medium, would convey purported messages from deceased loved ones either through a Ouija board or by automatic writing, even directly through the medium's vocal chords. Often the motive was to provide emotional comfort for the bereft. It has to be said the practice was largely fake, a sport of sorts in which self-proclaimed psychics

English Ouija

could earn kudos for gaining access to the supernatural world.

During some séances, claims were supported by the bizarre exudation of ectoplasm from the medium's orifices. Usually a white glue-like substance, sometimes even manifesting the facial features of a relevant person's spirit, oozed from ears, nostrils, even from between the legs. This ectoplasm was believed to be the materialization of a spirit in the material world and was taken to be proof of the existence of spirits.

Definitions

And so to return to the original question, what *is* meant by 'ghosts'? An apparition is a visible appearance of a person or animal or object that is not materially present. Apparitions are usually, though not necessarily, identified with spirits of the dead. Some appearances are of people still alive but displaced from the actual location of the person at the time. They usually last only a short time, and may appear and disappear without explanation.

When a person's 'double', or ghost of the living, appears it is sometimes called a wraith. In Celtic folklore the wraith is a herald of death and usually the person it represents is expected to die soon, or possibly has just done so. A phantom is often used as a synonym for ghost, but may also imply a subjective figment of a person's imagination. It can refer to a recurring ghostly object, such as a ship or coach, usually associated with a particular setting. A spectre is simply an appearance of the supernatural and is therefore another synonym for ghost or phantom. It does, however, sometimes carry the additional meaning of an evil premonition in the form of an illusory ghost.

Various cultures have their own terms for certain types of ghosts. In Russian folklore the Domovik is an ancestral spirit that dwells behind the stove in the home. He is grey-bearded and is like a guardian angel in that he protects the family from evil spirits and moves with them from house to house. However, if the family commit mischievous deeds, the Domovik is likely to react, often using forceful poltergeist activity, even to the extent of destroying the home.

Not all evidence of ghosts is visible. It can be audible, in the form of footsteps, rapping, vocal sounds such as groaning, weeping, screams, as might be associated with the past suffering of individuals. Poltergeists are a case in point.

Poltergeists

A ghost or energy that makes knocking noises or moves objects about a house is known as a poltergeist (from the German, *poltern*, 'to knock', and *geist*, 'ghost'). Because these movements often result in breakages, the spirits responsible are thought to be malevolent. Others believe they are merely mischievous nuisances. The noises may be bangs, thuds or rappings; the objects 'hurled' can range from small trinkets to large pieces of furniture. The phenomena thus described as poltergeist activity can range widely and carry a number of interpretations. Objects may appear to

Nandor Fodor

be directed at individuals living in a house, or the trajectory may seem strange and unnatural; some things, such as coins or stones, have rained down inside a house; fires have broken out spontaneously; electric lights switched on and off; telephone connections cut; objects, even people, have been said to levitate; some have been tapped on the shoulder, even assaulted, by scratching or pinching; and sometimes liquids are involved, such as oozing blood or water. Curiously wherever poltergeists are reported they seldom turn into apparitions.

Poltergeist activity has been a known phenomenon ever since ancient times. They were regarded as emanations of evil spirits, and usually attributed to people believed to have demonic possession such as witches. In a famous case in 18th century Britain the Reverend Samuel Wesley (whose sons John and Charles founded Methodism) was reputedly subjected to a poltergeist force in his home at Epworth Rectory. Mysterious rumblings, groans and vibrations frequently disturbed the household and were variously attributed to spirits and witchcraft. Reverend Wesley stood firm, resisting the advice to move house, and was duly vindicated as the noises suddenly and unaccountably stopped after a couple of months.

As psychical research became a serious investigation from the 19th century, more scientific explanations were explored. In the 1930s a psychoanalyst, Nandor Fodor, suggested that poltergeist phenomenon might result from individuals living in a dwelling who are suffering from intense psychological disturbance, such as repression or anger. According to this theory, a living person becomes the agent of such activity which is a sort of unconscious psycho-kinesis. Put simply, their negative emotions and thought processes actually produce the poltergeist effects. Yet, as William Roll of the Psychical Research Foundation in North Carolina asserts, these effects are not deliberate. A child or teenager, for example, who harbours anger as a result of family stress may periodically trigger a poltergeist-like action.

One of the more sensational cases of poltergeist activity is the Drummer of Tedworth in Wiltshire.

Drummer Of Tedworth

In 1661 the magistrate John Mompesson passed sentence on an itinerant conjuror, William Drury, for breach of the peace. He was banished from the area and his drum confiscated. Soon afterwards Mompesson suffered loud booming sounds in his house as though emitted from a drum. Other disturbances included moving objects, the levitating of his children from their beds, and animal noises. What was perceived at the time to be a curse Drury had laid on the magistrate is now regarded as a classic case of poltergeist activity.

THE ROSENHEIM POLTERGEIST

In November 1967 a bizarre series of disturbances in an office in Rosenheim, Bavaria, has become one of the most convincing cases of poltergeist activity ever recorded. Most of the phenomena involved electrical or telephonic equipment. Spontaneous explosions of light bulbs and fuses prompted an electrical engineer to inspect the power supply and circuitry. When nothing irregular was found, an independent power unit was installed to eliminate the possibility of fluctuations in the supply to the building. But the strange phenomena continued as before. All four telephone lines would sometimes ring when no one was actually calling in. Bills listed hundreds of calls out of the office that were never made, curiously often to the speaking clock.

More experts were brought in to investigate and they installed monitoring equipment. Then it was revealed that the disturbances occurred only during office hours and seemed to be connected with one employee, Annemarie Schneider, a 19 year-old clerk. Often the first power blip of the day would happen when she arrived at the office. Strategically placed cameras filmed lights going on and off above her head when she walked down the corridor. And bizarrely the monitoring equipment seemed, if anything, to increase the volume of abnormalities. Now drawers began to open of their own accord, pictures would fall off their wall hangings, filing cabinets were even said to shift across the floor.

No rational cause was ever found for the disturbances. Over 40 witnesses, including

Rosenheim Poltergeist

police officers, engineers, journalists, and parapsychologists, were involved in what became one of the best attested cases of poltergeist haunting ever recorded. Yet all the 'symptoms' of poltergeist activity stopped immediately Annemarie Schneider left her employment there. This undeniable association led some to conclude that the office in Rosenheim had become the object of 'spontaneous telekinesis'. Through a telekinetic link, psychic energy emanating from the employee had activated a poltergeist.

Why do ghosts appear?

If poltergeists can be ascribed to some form of telekinesis, how do we explain the more traditional experiences of ghosts, those fleeting apparitions? The reason widely held in ancient societies for returning to the land of the living was the need of a proper burial. It was said, for example that the ghost of the murdered Roman emperor Caligula haunted the Lamian Gardens where his ashes lay, until he had received a burial fitting for an emperor. Only then would his spirit be able to rest in peace.

Other reasons include the desire to offer guidance or warning to the living who find themselves in a perilous situation, or conversely to avenge a past wrongdoing. The Roman poet Ovid describes the spectre of Remus returning to haunt his adversary in a bid for justice.

Some ghosts are said to return to a place which their corporeal counterpart once loved or hated, or had some close association with. In some cases the ghost appears to have wished to relieve itself of the burden of guilt carried over from earthly existence.

In the Middle Ages ghosts were sometimes described as 'revenants', spirits that reappear in order to deliver messages about the condition of the departed soul. During the Reformation in Europe Roman Catholics and Protestants would argue about the meaning of apparitions. Catholics believed ghosts were telling us their souls were trapped in purgatory (an ethereal realm where souls are temporarily held pending judgement), and that they needed our help to activate their release; while Protestants regarded apparitions as solely the evil manifestations of the devil. As secular streams of thought emerged in the 18th century, testimonies of ghostly phenomena were increasingly appraised independently of religious doctrinal views. Undoubtedly sightings of spirits exerted a tremendous interest in various sectors of society, from playwrights to gothic novelists to amateur spiritualists, and in time, to serious psychic researchers and parapsychologists of the 20th century. One of the problems of investigating ghosts is that they are nearly always seen only by one person at a time, so the study necessarily becomes one of ghost *experience* rather than of ghosts per se. For this reason the scientific establishment has in the main stopped short of becoming involved in such investigations. However, the Society for Psychical Research, founded in 1882, aimed to conduct research in

Edmund Gurney

Frederick Myers

Henry Sidgwick

as scientific a manner as the subject would allow. The organization was set up by three researchers at Trinity College, Cambridge: Edmund Gurney, Frederick Myers and Henry Sidgwick. Within a few years, an offshoot formed in the US. Together they have investigated numerous claims, as much to eliminate hoaxes as to corroborate the genuine, including such extraordinary cases as Ballechin House and Raynham Hall, both of which are covered in this book. The organization still thrives. It produces a quarterly publication, *Journal of the Society for Psychical Research*, and holds an annual conference. Its avowed aim is to 'understand events and abilities commonly described as "psychic" or "paranormal" by promoting and supporting important research in this area'.

On the fringe

Some people point to certain subliminal experiences, such as Out of Body Experiences (OBE) and Deathbed Visions, as evidence for the existence of, if not exactly ghosts, then a parallel spiritual world. While sceptics argue that an OBE is merely the result of an altered state of consciousness, those who actually have had the experience tend to believe they have 'visited' a distinctly different realm. Furthermore, this phenomenon – in which a person feels he or she has separated from their physical body and has witnessed an unearthly realm – is thought to have been experienced by as many as one in four people. Common to most reports of an OBE is the sensation of being in a second body, a ghostly double of the physical body. This second body, sometimes referred to as the Doppelgänger, is usually invisible to others, though some reports have sensed its presence in a room or even witnessed it as an apparition. The experience, often described as something fantastic, may occur during sleep or when perfectly awake. It may happen at times of stress or severe illness, or can be induced by hypnosis or meditation. Some who believe in the authenticity of OBEs have speculated that these departures of the consciousness from the physical body may go some way to explaining the presence of spiritual entities at large in the physical world.

Visions from the dying of glowing light and dead figures known to the person are a well-attested phenomenon across many cultures. Typically a person dying from a terminal illness over a period of time rather than from quick death may glimpse scenes associated with an afterlife, such as a beautiful garden. Many have apparitions of deceased loved ones, some of religious figures such as the Virgin Mary. Although there is a strong religious theme of life after death evinced from these experiences, which sceptics attribute to a form of wish fulfilment, deathbed visions are as likely to occur to non-believers as to those who believe in heaven. The visions also happen to those who wish ardently to recover from their illness. Some explanations have been given on medical grounds, attributing the cause to the hallucinatory effect of drugs or fever. Yet an extensive study of the phenomenon in the US in 1960 by Karl Osis of the American Society for Psychical Research indicated that deathbed visions were more likely to occur when the patient was fully conscious and were not induced by medical treatment. A curious additional phenomenon observed by friends and relatives visiting the sick has been a silvery 'mist' of energy floating over the body prior to death. Is it possible that these experiences are allied to those that are claimed to be apparitions of ghosts?

HAUNTED HOUSES

Rebel Hack of Toronto
Mackenzie House and things that go slap in the night

William Lyon Mackenzie

William Lyon Mackenzie (1795–1861) was a radical newspaper editor who led a failed rebellion in 1837 and was convicted of high treason. He was also Toronto's first mayor and grandfather of the future prime minister of Canada, William Lyon Mackenzie King.

Mackenzie emigrated from Scotland in 1820 at the age of 25. He set up a newspaper, the *Colonial Advocate*, and campaigned for political independence from Great Britain. After failing in a rebellion against the mother country a ten-year exile to the US seemed to spell the end of Mackenzie's career.

But his return to Canada in 1850 was greeted with rapturous joy. Political supporters expressed their admiration for the brave pioneer by building a grand house for the Scot, his wife Isabel and their 13 children. Designed in fashionable Georgian style, the house stood in the heart of Toronto at 82 Bond Street. Alas within two years of moving in, William Mackenzie was dead, breathing his last in bed.

The distraught Isabel eventually sold the house. By the 1930s it had deteriorated and was due to be demolished. But the prime minister of the time, William Lyon Mackenzie King, being related to the original owner and proud of his efforts to win independence, ordered the house to be restored.

A couple, Mr and Mrs Dobban, were appointed caretakers in 1960. It was only when they had taken residence that strange things began to happen at 82 Bond Street. Unaccountable sounds were heard in the house. At night, footsteps went up the stairs, yet no one was living there. On another night they woke to a cranking noise in the basement. Thinking it might be the oil burner, Mr Dobban checked but found it to be cold. They reckoned the noise must have been coming from the old press, which used to print the *Colonial Advocate*, locked in one of the adjacent rooms in the basement. On some nights even the sound of music could be heard coming from the front room where there was a piano.

After a month, Mrs Dobban couldn't stand it any longer and the couple moved out. They were replaced by a no-nonsense couple, Mr and Mrs Edmund. On the very night they moved in they heard the same footsteps on the stairs. Increasingly they felt the presence of something in the house, yet nothing was ever seen … until one particular night when Mrs Edmunds woke suddenly feeling something touching her shoulder. She opened her eyes to see the clear form of a woman peering

down at her, yet it was no one she knew personally. Indeed Mrs Edmund 'knew' instinctively it was a ghost. It had long brown hair which hung down in front of her shoulders, and a narrow face. After a few moments the phantom disappeared and did not return for two years. This time it seemed to come in vengeance, for according to Mrs Edmund's report, the ghost reached out and slapped the caretaker's wife across the face leaving a black eye and bruised cheekbone, such was the force of the strike.

Another ghostly sighting involved a small bald man in a frock coat. Again, he would be seen only for a few seconds before disappearing. At other times the two figures were seen standing in a room on the third floor.

Mr Edmunds claimed never to witness either of the ghosts, only the sounds. But his grandchildren, when once staying there, were terrified one night when they saw a strange woman appear in the bathroom while getting ready for bed.

The woman seen in various parts of the house is thought to be Isabel, Mackenzie's wife.

An exorcism was performed on the

house. Afterwards a third caretaker, Mrs Winifred McCleary, complained the air was still 'oppressive' and heard unusual nosies such as a toilet flush when no one was in the bathroom. A second exorcism was undertaken, this time with a more successful outcome.

No one has lived in the Mackenzie house since 1967, and now it has been turned into a museum of sorts.

A Harvard professor, William Kilbourn, wrote a biography of Mackenzie, entitled *Firebrand*, and was convinced the witness accounts are true. Subsequent experiences of visitors have included strange sightings of orb lights, voices and sensations of figures present.

Noose of Yankee Jim
Convict's return to Whaley House

One of the most haunted houses in North America is the Whaley House in San Diego. To look at it you would think it a fine place to live, a two storey chalet-style home with balcony and veranda and a wonderful view of the bay at San Francisco. Indeed at the time it was thought to be one of the finest houses in southern California. Prominent members of society in Old Town San Diego would come to parties there. there was even a small theatre upstairs. The place was so spacious the government leased some of the rooms on an occasional basis, one of them used as a courtroom.

It turns out that the site chosen by Thomas Whaley, a fortune hunter in the great Californian goldrush, was once the scene of a hanging. A gallows set up on the back of a wagon ended the days of a renegade sailor, Yankee Jim Robinson, who was convicted of theft. The spot is said to coincide precisely with an archway now separating the sitting room from the music room in Whaley House.

Indeed Thomas Whaley even witnessed the death, though it did not put him off building a home there. After the family moved into their luxurious new residence, heavy footsteps were heard clumping about the house at night. It was thought they might belong to Yankee Jim, returned to seek his revenge.

Subsequent disturbances in the former courtroom took the form of

noisy meetings and occasional uproar.
And once, in the dead of night, the
ghostly image of Whaley's deceased
wife, Anna, was seen hovering
between the music and sitting rooms.

Investigation

In 1966 a group of psychic
investigators obtained permission
to spend the night there and try to
detect these ghostly phenomena.
Come late evening and the wife of
one of the reporters had to be taken
away having witnessed something
unspeakable on the upper floor.
All departed before dawn in a
state of high anxiety, some saying
they had seen the ghost of Yankee
Jim protesting the horror of his
punishment. A photographic archive
of the house reveals one shot of the
archway between the music and
sitting rooms containing the outline

Whaley House

of a noose suspended beneath it – no
doubt the one that broke poor Yankee
Jim's neck.

Distraught Nun
Strange energy at Borley Rectory

Once reputed to be England's
most haunted house, Borley
Rectory near Sudbury in Essex has
a mysterious past rooted in an illicit
love affair. Long before the Victorian
rectory was built, a Benedictine
monastery existed on the site. One
of the monks is said to have seduced
a local nun. Before they had time to
elope the two lovers were caught and
punished – he with execution, she
with incarceration in the cellar.

It is said that the rectory's first
incumbent, Reverend Bull, built a
summerhouse overlooking a garden
with an overgrown path running
through known as Nun's Walk. He
claimed sometimes to be able to
see the form of a distraught woman
wandering the garden near this path,
apparently looking for someone.

Knowing the background, Bull
considered this must be a ghostly

Borely Rectory

return of the nun longing for her lost lover. Bull would invite guests to join him in a ghost-watch, though none stayed long enough to experience anything. His children once claimed to see a woman at the window of a downstairs bedroom, and frequently spotted the apparition floating across the lawn, to their great astonishment.

So far there seemed nothing too sinister in the occasional appearance of a rather sorrowful ghost. But gradually matters became more

threatening – spectres appeared with great energy, especially once the rector had passed away.

When a dreadful horse-drawn coach rushed across the lawn accompanying the ghostly nun, the children, now grown, decided enough was enough and took their leave. Their successors, Reverend Eric Smith and his wife had not long taken their place when they experienced some unnerving poltergeist activity.

Harry Price investigates

An expert ghost-hunter, Harry Price, was invited to conduct an investigation. His first night there was lively enough. Together with the Reverend Smith, his wife and a newspaper reporter, the group became witnesses to a series of very strange happenings:

We were standing in the Summer House at dusk watching the lawn when I saw the 'apparition' which so many claim to have seen, but owing to the deep shadows it was impossible for one to discern any definite shape or attire. But something certainly moved along the path on the other side of the lawn and although I quickly ran across to investigate, it had vanished when I reached the place.

(Daily Mirror, 14 June 1929)

However, it was what happened next that really started to ring alarm bells. Harry Price continued:

As we strolled towards the rectory discussing the figure there came a terrific crash and a pane of glass from the roof of a porch hurtled to the ground. We ran inside and upstairs to inspect the room

immediately over the porch but found nobody. A few seconds later we were descending the stairs, when something flew past my head, hit an iron stove in the hall and shattered. With our flash lamps we inspected the broken pieces and found them to be sections of a red vase which, with its companion, had been standing on the mantelpiece of what is known as the Blue Room.

Determined to see through their investigation, the group spent a vigil in the rectory from 1 am to 4 am. The rector decided to address the 'presence' and received some interesting replies. Ghostly fingers tapped out messages on a mirror in the room where they were assembled, a bar of soap slammed down on a jug, and vases crashed against walls.

Naturally Borley Rectory became headline news, and further investigations were conducted. One of these took the form of a séance at which the mysterious nun appeared, identifying herself as one Marie Lairre. She said she had been strangled on May 17, 1667, and was buried in the garden. No remains have been found, but at another séance, in 1938, an unseen spirit announced that the rectory would burn down that night. The evening passed without further ado and the next morning the rectory stood as normal. But the following year, when the rectory was under new ownership, a lamp fell, apparently of its own accord, and set light to the place. As the fire raged, onlookers were aghast to see silhouetted against one of the windows the unmistakeable face of a nun.

The Haunted Cottage
Jung's disturbed nights

The famous psychologist Carl Jung spent a lifetime collating and analysing experiences connected with the paranormal. After delivering a paper entitled 'The Psychological Foundation of Belief in Spirits' to the Society of Psychical Research in 1919, he went on a lecture tour in Britain to express his ideas. He concluded that belief in spirits had three sources: apparitions, dreams, and 'pathological disturbances of psychic life'. He suggested that when somebody dies images and thoughts remain in the minds of loved ones

and are activated by the intensity of grief to form spirits, which are therefore psychological entities.

While in Britain, Jung stayed in a vacant cottage to be alone with his thoughts and prepare his lectures. Over the first few days a powerful unpleasant odour permeated the bedroom, though with no clear source. The following weekend the smell returned, though this time accompanied by a rustling noise like the swish of crinoline against a wall. Days later louder noises disturbed his work: rapping, crackling and banging, again with no apparent cause.

Then, on the final night of his stay at the cottage, an extraordinary happening capped the entire experience. While asleep on his bed, something caused him to wake up. There beside him he saw the image of an old woman lying on the bed, her face partly dissipated in the pillow.

Far from being afraid of these strange occurrences, Jung put them down to psychological causes. The smell in the room reminded him of a former patient who was similar to the old lady he saw in his vision - for that, he stressed, was all she was, not a

Carl Jung

ghostly reality. He believed the noises were mere imaginings prompted by drowsiness.

Green Lady's Walk
Longleat's restless spirit

One of England's most elegant stately houses is reputedly home to the ghost of the Marchioness of Weymouth. A top-floor corridor is known as the Green Lady's Walk, after sightings of Lady Louisa Carteret, grief-stricken wife of Thomas Thynne, second Viscount Weymouth.

Her longing in fact was not for her husband but for her lover who was so cruelly murdered.

The story begins early in the 18th century when Lady Louisa married the viscount who quickly developed an animosity, full of spite, towards her. The marriage was a disaster and before long the marchioness turned her attentiion elsewhere and fell in love with another man.

Unfortunately for the lovers, one day they were caught in bed together. Accounts vary as to how her humiliated husband reacted. One version says he burst into a rage and strangled the lover, another that he took the customary course and challenged him to a duel. Either way, the lover was killed and buried beneath the flagstones of the cellar. Four centuries later a man's skeleton wearing 18th century boots was indeed exhumed from the cellar floor when heating was due to be installed.

Lady Louisa died in childbirth in 1736 and ever since is believed to haunt the long corridor of the top floor of Longleat, pining for her stricken lover.

Longleat

Investigation

In 1965 an American TV crew
conducted a series of investigations
into haunted stately houses in Britain
and explored the shadowy parts of
this Elizabethan mansion. Apparently
the cameras managed to capture an
unearthly glowing light emitted from
a door on to the corridor. A bead
of light moved haphazardly some
10 metres along the corridor before
disappearing through another door.

Other mysterious lights appeared
on film but without apparent source,
and weird occurrences bothered the
TV crew. Plugs jumped out of sockets
during filming at key moments, and
some of the results turned out to
be darkly obscure when plenty of
lighting was employed. Other reports
have described a 'cloying, oppressive'
atmosphere in the corridor; some
even of keys turning in locked doors.

Quaking at Willington Mill
Christian family endure strange spirits

A good Quaker family of
Northumberland had their faith
severely tested in 1835 when they
moved into a mill house in Willington
village. The father, Joseph Proctor,
was an intelligent, devout Christian
who had no tolerance for any kind
of superstition.

Following the normal routine, a
nursemaid was putting their three
children to bed one bitterly cold
evening in January. They slept in
the nursery on the second floor. As
the nurse was going about her duty
she heard footsteps in the empty
room above. At first she assumed
they must belong to a handyman
doing some late maintenance and
thought nothing of it. But when she
mentioned it later to Mr Proctor, he
assured her no one was doing any
work at that hour and made light of
it saying this was an old house and
occasional noises were to be expected.
But when the same thing happened
the following night and the footsteps

continued for several minutes, the nurse immediately reported it to the owner.

Proctor decided to inspect the attic room, though for years the door to it had been nailed shut and its window boarded up. Inside, a fine layer of soot and dust lay on the floor, yet completely undisturbed.

Nevertheless the owner refused to consider any ideas of a haunting. That is, until he himself experienced something strange. He was conducting prayers one morning in the front parlour when heavy footfall was heard coming down the stairs, through the hall to the front door. The bolts were drawn back and the lock turned. Proctor raised himself and went out into the hall, but the surprise meant he was slow to react, though he followed the sound as best he could. Footsteps went down the path and disappeared, and Mrs Proctor promptly fainted.

The family were at a loss as to what they could do. Domestic servants were leaving out of fear. Indeed only one loyal girl, Mary Young, who had been with them from long back, stayed on. But there seemed no respite from disturbance. If anything, noises became more frequent and varied. Thumps, the creak of doors opening, chairs scraping on floorboards, even the sound of heavy breathing, were all heard. And indeed all the disturbance was only by sound. No one as yet had *seen* anything. But that was about to change.

Determined not to let these strange happenings get the better of them, the Proctor family tried to carry on life as normally as they could. But when Mrs Proctor invited her two sisters to stay at Whitsun, even the calmest of nerves would jangle.

The sisters visit
Choosing to sleep together, they felt on the very first night the four-poster bed on which they lay judder unaccountably. The following night the movement was more pronounced, violent even, the curtains opened and closed, as though something had passed between them. Not wishing to cut short their visit, having journeyed for some considerable time from their home, the sisters persevered. But then for the first time, a sighting was experienced.

As they lay in bed, unable to sleep of course, a terrifying apparition occurred: from within the opposite wall emerged an obscure bluish figure of a woman. She – it – approached and leaned over the bed. Speechless with terror, the sisters dared not move a tissue, could hardly even dare breathe. After what seemed an age, though probably only a few moments, the spectre receded to whence it came forth.

Needless to say, neither sister stayed another night in that room. One left altogether, the other moved next door to stay with the mill foreman and his wife. They too had witnessed strange things outside the house, noises on the gravel path, and so on. Indeed one night, they and their daughter had seen a luminous figure drifting about the upper floor of the house, seemingly dressed in a priest's surplice. It then turned and looked out of the window directly towards the place where they stood.

Calling in the ghostbuster

Deciding enough was enough, Proctor agreed to call in an amateur 'ghostbuster', Dr Edward Drury.

Many of the cases he investigated turned out to be hoaxes, and he arrived with his assistant Mr Hudson fully expecting this one to be no different. Proctor took the precaution of sending his family away while the two investigators did their surveillance. Camped on the third floor landing outside the haunted room, Dr Drury and his friend listened intently for tell-tale evidence. And sure enough at around midnight, the sound of feet and knocking on floorboards began.

They held their position to see if anything else would happen. All went quiet, for about half an hour nothing was heard. Dr Drury was about to retire downstairs when suddenly the closet door opposite him opened. The figure of a woman emerged, just as the two sisters had experienced, except this time she, or it, was draped in grey cloths. The ghost moved towards Mr Hudson. In a state of high anxiety, Dr Drury determined to encounter the thing and charged at it, not knowing what might happen. Yet nothing did 'happen' as such. Dr Drury simply passed through like thin air. The ghoul vanished and did not reappear. Mr Hudson raised the alarm and with the help of Proctor carried the terrified doctor downstairs. Some days later, when he had recovered, Dr Drury admitted to have gone to Willington Mill a sceptic, but come away a convinced believer in the supernatural.

Canine spirits at Ballechin
Scotland's mysterious manor

A manor house in Tayside that belonged to the Stuart family became the subject of a mysterious haunting after its owner, Major Robert Stuart, returned from overseas service in India. While abroad, the officer had come to believe in reincarnation and, furthermore, in the migration of souls between animal and human. His avowed intention was to return to Ballechin House after his death in the form of his beloved black spaniel.

When the major died in 1876 the house passed to his nephew, John Stuart. Nervous that his uncle's belief may come true, that his soul may incarnate in one of the dogs there, he

ordered all the hounds to be shot.

Soon after Robert's death strange events were reported in the house under its new owners. One day John's wife was carrying out some administrative tasks in what used to be the major's study and noticed an unusual smell of dogs. She opened the window to freshen the air and then felt a frightening rub on her leg as though an invisible hound had brushed against her.

Some days later inexplicable sounds were heard: gunfire, argument, and noises from the master bedroom, all of which had no logical explanation. Of course once news of these strange happenings reached the village, the house soon acquired a reputation for being haunted.

A theory spread that Robert Stuart's spirit was disturbed and, frustrated in its disembodied state, had returned to haunt Ballechin.

John's children became so frightened that a new wing had to be built to house them away from the haunted zone. A friend of the family and Jesuit priest came to stay and he too heard the various noises described. Alas, after living there for some 20 years, the family suffered a tragic bereavement when John was run down by a cab while crossing a road in London. His death spelled the end of their time at Ballechin and the house was rented out. However, new tenants complained of ghostly paraphernalia similar to what the Stuarts had experienced, with poltergeist activity as well.

Investigation

Once the house became empty a team of psychic researchers under the leadership of the Marquis of Bute moved in to conduct an investigation. Almost immediately they too heard sounds of loud clanging, of gunfire and voices. A Ouija board was set up to try to gain some sort of spiritual directive to what was going on.

In one session the name of Ishbel came up – Robert Stuart's sister, a devout Roman Catholic who became a nun after her brother's death, was called Isabel. The spirit of Ishbel, who was thus identified with Isabel, led the Ouija party outside to a garden pond. There all the participants were amazed to behold the figure of a nun in black habit strolling through the

woods before disappearing.

However, no conclusions were ever drawn about the canine spirit allegedly haunting Ballechin. The house was eventually demolished in the 1960s.

Ghost of the Tulip Staircase
National Maritime Museum, Greenwich, 1966

A couple of Canadian tourists could hardly have expected to cause such a sensation with their camera when they came to London in 1966. A retired clergyman, Ralph Hardy, and his wife decided to visit the famous 17th century Queen's House designed by Inigo Jones, home to the National Maritime Museum.

Although the house had no history of any haunting, a photograph taken by Mr Hardy clearly shows the form of a wraith climbing the bottom of the ornate Tulip Staircase. Two hands are visibly gripping the hand rail and a female form in perhaps a white nightgown is discernible. Yet the Hardys swear that no one was present at the time – they simply wished to capture the beauty of the serpentine staircase. Kodak examined the film and confirmed that there had been no tampering with the negative.

Subsequently, museum staff who were questioned about the occasion remembered seeing strange figures about the staircase, some even claimed to hear the faint sound of footfall.

In May 2002, staff observed the form of a woman wearing a diaphanous crinoline dress drifting along the open landing of Queen's House before vanishing into a wall.

Appeasing Ghosts of Winchester
The antics of San Francisco's eccentric millionairess

One of the features of the American Civil War was the novel use of a 'repeating' rifle, one that could fire successive shots without needing to reload. The firearm was named the Winchester Repeating Rifle after the man who invented it, Oliver Winchester.

His son, William, married during the Civil War but he and his wife, Sarah, lost their new born, and only

child, a month after its birth. Some years later, William himself died, leaving a large fortune to his wife.

Sarah found it near impossible to overcome her grief and was advised that this may be because the sprit of her late husband was trying to contact her. So she conducted séances to see if she could gain access to his spirit, but without success.

Then one medium from Boston, Adam Coons, suggested that she might have fallen under a curse because of the multiple deaths caused by the Winchester rifle. Indeed the deaths of her child and husband could equally be attributed to the same cause. The only solution was to placate these wounded spirits.

Laying the ghosts
So in a bizarre series of events, Sarah set her mind to doing just that. She followed the instruction apparently given by William's spirit to sell her home in New Haven, move to the West, and build a new house for herself and all the ghosts of those who fell to the Winchester rifle in the war.

Sarah spent the rest of her life, 33

years, building, extending and altering a house to suit what she perceived to be the spirits' requirements. The result was an extraordinary idiosyncrasy based loosely on a Victorian style. She became obsessed with the number 13: each room had 13 windows, 13 lights, 13 cupboards, and no mirrors were allowed. In all there were 160 rooms, but access to them was limited and tortuous. Stairways were designed to lead nowhere, doors opened on to bare walls.

The widow seldom left the house and lived there until the age of 82. She was said to hold dinner parties for her ghostly guests in her secret 'blue' room. On her death the strange abode, left to her niece, was sold. Now the Winchester Mystery House is open to the public as a tourist attraction.

Raynham Hall
'Brown Lady' with the lamp

The Walpole family became famous for its politicians of the 18th century, Robert being Britain's first Prime Minister. But his sister, Dorothy, diverted their fame in a

new direction when she gained a reputation for haunting the home of her late husband, Viscount Charles Townshend.

Their marriage in 1713 turned sour when the proud baron discovered Dorothy had had a premarital affair with a notorious philanderer. Her punishment was incarceration in their home at Raynham Hall, Norfolk, for the rest of her life. She was forbidden to see any of her children, and allegedly died at the age of 40, some say of smallpox, others from falling down a staircase – and no accident either. Yet others at the time maintained the funeral was a fake and that Dorothy continued to live into old age.

In later years a series of apparitions of a 'Brown Lady' were reported in the Hall. She is said to wear a dress made of brown brocade and often carries a lamp. Most fearful are her empty eye sockets. Once George IV, no less, was staying there and after being awakened in the night by a white lady dressed in brown he made a hasty departure the next morning complaining the house was 'cursed'.

A Colonel Loftus said he spotted

her twice at Christmas in 1835, and alerted the police who conducted an investigation, but to no avail. A Victorian novelist, Captain Marryat, was so alarmed at the sight of the dreadful spectre he fired his gun at it, only to see the bullets perforate the wall behind.

This shooting seemed to frighten the ghost away for some time, for it was not until 1926 that the next sighting of Dorothy was recorded. Like Colonel Loftus's experience, Marquess Townshend, then a boy, claimed to see a phantom on the staircase, believed to be the very site of her death resulting from Lord Townshend throwing her down.

Then sensationally the spectral presence appeared for the first time in a photograph taken by Indra Shira of *Country Life* magazine. The picture shows the misty outline of a shrouded woman descending the stairs. According to royal staff, Queen Elizabeth has seen the figure too; apparently it makes her corgis bark violently. Likewise in the 1950s a ghost hunter sat up all night in the hope of catching a glimpse and saw nothing, but his dogs woke

and appeared to become extremely frightened by something. Although the figure has not been seen of late within the house, some reports claim sight of her on the road nearby.

CASTLES AND PALACES

Headless Boleyn
Henry VIII's wife in Bloody Tower

Of the many illustrious ghouls that grace the grounds and apartments of London's famous

Anne Boleyn

Bloody Tower, none has been spotted more often than the ghost of Anne Boleyn. The second wife of Henry VIII was beheaded there for alleged adultery in 1536 and is said to have been seen, with head in hand, by several different witnesses on separate occasions. She is said to haunt the White Tower, the King's House and Tower Green. The queen is reported to have led a spectral procession through the Chapel of St Peter, where her headless body is buried in an arrow case beneath the flagstones. In the 19th century a guard believed he was suddenly confronted by her figure in an aggressive stance. Fearing for his life, he charged and ran his bayonet directly through the eerie apparition, which proved to have no material substance, causing him to faint on the spot.

Thomas Becket murder

The Two Princes, *reputedly murdered on the orders of the future Richard III, have been seen holding hands on the staircase and are said to still haunt the Tower today;* Catherine Howard, *beheaded fifth wife of Henry VIII, whose screams have been heard as she begs for mercy;* Lady Jane Grey, *whose hands are claimed to have clasped a Yeoman Warder's throat in the Salts Tower;* Sir Walter Raleigh, *incarcerated for 13 years before his execution during the reign of James I, apparently became visible to Tower Guardsmen in 1864.*

ILLUSTRIOUS GALLERY

Other ghosts seen at the Tower are: **Thomas Becket,** *the murdered archbishop of Canterbury, whose sighting so terrified Henry II's grandson, Henry III, that he abandoned building an inner curtain wall at the Tower and built a chapel instead;*

Omen of Doom
White Lady of Hohenzollern

The Hohenzollern Dynasty ruled the Holy Roman Empire for 400 years, its power extending over Prussia, Germany and Romania. Associated with this royal house was the White Lady, a spectre that emerged at key moments in history to give counsel on impending events. Only once is she believed to have actually voiced such advice. It came in 1628 when these words in Latin were heard: *'Veni judica vivos et mortuos'* (I come to judge the living

and the dead). A young prince of Hohenzollern died shortly afterwards.

One of the mightiest of the Holy Roman electors was Frederick the Great of Prussia, yet the White Lady never appeared to him, at least not while he was alive. When his nephew, Frederick William II, was encamped outside Paris preparing to lay siege to the French capital, the deceased Frederick the Great is said to have made a timely appearance warning his nephew not to attack or he will suffer the punishment of the White Lady. Frederick William was so struck by the force of his uncle's message that

Hohenzollern

he immediately called off his troops and retreated from France.

He, therefore, escaped the wrath of this spectral lady, but his successors were not so lucky. Both Frederick William III, in 1840, and Frederick William IV, in 1860, received omens of their imminent deaths.

The ghost became well known in a number of German castles, including those at Berlin, Neuhaus, Tretzen and Raumleau. She is said to appear in white robes and to wear a widow's band round her head. It is believed that she may be related to the 15th century Princess Bertha, whom her husband, the cruel Baron Steyermark, treated abhorrently, and has lived on in spirit ever since to take revenge on future Hohenzollern rulers.

WHITE LADIES

Common as a type of ghost to haunt several castles of Britain and elsewhere is the White Lady. Often she is the spectre of a noblewoman who suffered in her lifetime, usually was murdered or died tragically, and returns to haunt the descendants of her lineage as a harbinger of doom. Typically white ladies drift along corridors and pathways, sometimes holding a cup of poison. In France they are usually considered to be beautiful and sometimes seen near bridges. In this context the association is with the medieval custom of sacrificing girls to river spirits whose placation thus allows villagers to cross the river in safety.

Long Beard of Glamis
The world's most haunted castle

The ancestral home of the late Queen Mother, Elizabeth Bowes-Lyon, is the oldest inhabited castle in Scotland. It was also the setting for Shakespeare's blood-thirsty play, *Macbeth*, and is reputed to be one of the most haunted castles in the world. Indeed, for that reason many legends have spawned here and it is difficult to distinguish between fiction and genuine experience.

In times of clan warfare, tales spread of betrayed men walled up in the dungeon and their spirits haunting the castle. Several of the 90 rooms have been the scene of dreadful deeds, including the murder of King

Malcolm II, the likely inspiration for the same fate of Duncan, Thane of Glamis, in *Macbeth*. Queen Elizabeth II has admitted to seeing a ghostly Grey Lady that is reported to roam spooky corridors. The novelist Sir Walter Scott felt distinctly uncomfortable while staying there, and decided to curtail his visit to one night only.

But the most compelling account of supernatural activity at Glamis comes from Lord Halifax, British ambassador to the US in the 1940s, and brother-in-law to the castle's owner. So disturbed was he by the experience of a Mrs Monro, guest of the owners Lord and Lady Strathmore in 1869, that he wrote extensively about it in *The Ghost Book*.

His description runs:

In the middle of the night, Mrs Monro awoke with a sensation as though someone was bending over her; indeed, I have heard that she felt a beard brush her face. The night-light having gone out, she called her husband to get up and find the matches. In the pale glimmer of the winter moon she saw a figure pass into the dressing room.

The account describes how the couple heard a terrible scream from their young child in the dressing room. They rushed in to find him in great distress saying he had seen a giant. As they calmed him in their bed, a loud crash was then heard, followed by the clock chiming four.

Glamis Castle

Knowing their hosts to be nervous of hearing about strange occurrences at the castle, the couple agreed to keep quiet about what had happened when they went down to breakfast the next morning. However, when another couple staying there promptly described a similar experience, which happened at the same time, Mrs Monro could not contain herself and blurted out their story too.

The following night everyone heard the same loud crash, and once again only moments before the clock struck four. Nothing more was heard.

Lord Halifax's dream

Strange enough events, yet things were about to get stranger still. One night Lord Halifax dreamt he was staying at Glamis and was chased by a giant with a long beard. In the ensuing struggle Halifax became aware his opponent had dead eyes but was no enemy as such. Indeed, when Halifax offered him some 'broken chains' which the maid had retrieved from a lower chamber, the giant was grateful to his benefactor, saying, 'You have lifted a great weight off me … those irons have been weighing me

down ever since 1486'.

A curious date, thought Halifax. It turns out that on the very same night that Halifax had this dream a guest staying at Glamis awoke to see a ghost sitting on her bed, a large man with a beard staring at her with dead eyes.

When Halifax later learned of this apparition from Lady Strathmore, the coincidence was made the more astounding when she heard of the date revealed in Halifax's dream. For the most sinister ghost ever to haunt Glamis was Earl Beardie, murdered in that year of 1486.

Caught on Camera
Spooks at Hampton Court

Inevitably a palace in which two of Henry VIII's unfortunate wives lived is bound to be associated with ghost stories. Jane Seymour, who died after giving birth to Henry's only son Edward, has been seen dressed in white carrying a candle about the state apartments of this rambling Tudor castle. Henry's fifth wife, Catherine Howard, charged with adultery five years later, has been heard many times shrieking to her husband in an effort to obtain a last-minute reprieve. The passage is named the Haunted Gallery in her honour.

Other, non-royal figures are also said to haunt the palace, such as Edward's nurse, Sybil Penn, who is known as the Grey Lady and is sometimes seen at a spinning wheel.

More alarming – and recently captured on video film – was an occurrence in October 2003. Security guards were alerted to an open fire door but on examining closed-circuit cameras the door was observed to be violently flung open yet there was no one at the scene. The following day an extraordinary vision was caught on film of a ghostly figure in robes in the doorway. One arm reached for the door handle and closed the door. His face appeared quite white and unnatural. A member of security interviewed after watching the footage said, 'It was incredibly spooky because the face didn't look human'. A spokeswoman for the Palace claimed it was definitely no hoax, and that they genuinely had no idea who or what it was.

Monarchs of Windsor
From the graceful to the insane

Great Windsor Castle, originally built by William the Conqueror, has been the home to ghosts of at least four English monarchs. The figure of Henry VIII is reported to have moved sluggishly about certain parts, clearly still suffering from his ulcerous leg. As recently as 1918, a Guards officer who was reading alone in the Castle library one evening claimed to have seen the ghost of Elizabeth I pass noiselessly before him. In fact this part of the castle was one of the few that the queen had built and decorated. More recently still, Princess Margaret also confided in friends that she too had encounters with the Tudor queen's ghost and with a phantom of the beheaded Charles I.

The fourth monarch recorded here in ghostly form is George III. He is said often to be sighted in the library muttering over ancient books. One sentry's personal experience of the mad king is contained in Hector Bolitho's *The Romance of Windsor.*

Windsor Castle at sunset

Long after George III died, the sentry on the terrace looked up at the window one evening and saw a hand parting the curtains. The ghost of George III looked down at the soldier, and a pale hand was raised to the salute. The curtains fell back and the terrified soldier ran to his companion on the East Terrace. Soldiers came to hate their vigil on the North Terrace, for the ghost appeared again and again, until the death of William IV when the Hanoverian regime ended and the ghost apparently retired into tranquility.

Hector Bolitho, *The Romance of Windsor* (London, c.1943)

Windsor Great Park

Of older tradition is the haunting of Windsor Great Park, in which Richard II's forester, Herne the Hunter, was believed to roam, having committed suicide by hanging himself from a tree. Our knowledge of the story comes chiefly from Shakespeare in *The Merry Wives of Windsor*:

There is an old tale goes, that Herne the hunter,
Sometimes a keeper here in Windsor Forest,
Doth all the winter time, at still

midnight,

Walk round about an oak, with great ragg'd horns;

And there he blasts the trees, and takes the cattle,

And makes milch kine [milking cows] yield blood, and shakes

A chain

In a most hideous and dreadful manner.

A traditional belief holds that suicides haunt the place of their death. His rattling chain is a common motif of spectral apparitions. But the 'ragg'd' horns, meaning those of a stag, probably identify him as Cernunnos, the antlered Celtic god of the underworld. Also unusual are the activities of withering trees, bewitching cattle and causing cow's milk to turn to blood. Legend has it that this royal huntsman belonged to this ancient forest long before any kings arrived and was adopted as a servant of the realm who tended to appear at times of national crisis.

Ghoulish Belles of Alabama
One couple's experience at Rocky Hill Castle

An old house in Courtland, Alabama, was for generations the home of the Saunders family. A fine mansion, Rocky Hill Castle, was erected by Reverend Saunders in 1828, and until the 1950s the Saunders' lived happily there, even with their family ghost.

When asked why they continued

Herne the Hunter

Rocky Hill Castle

Rocky Hill Castle

living there if the house was haunted, their answer was that they loved the place. Besides, the ghost never did them any harm.

The first sign of haunting was a mere clanking in the basement, a sound like the rattling of chains, on a few occasions. But when Mr Saunders' investigated, he saw or heard nothing out of the ordinary. At other times there was a tapping noise. Not enough to cause fear, but enough to make them inquisitive. What

the Saunders did know is that the builders of the castle had died there a long time ago.

Then Mrs Saunders started to feel the presence of someone or something in the room where she used to sit. But when she turned round no one was there, yet the feeling that she was being watched persisted. Eventually, being bothered so much by this sensation, she addressed the presence out loud, telling it to speak out or be gone. And believe it or not, Mrs Saunders heard a reply: 'Sister, do not be doubting, for I am truly here'.

In a somewhat nervous state, Mrs Saunders was later descending the stairs at their home to suddenly behold a vision of a woman dressed in the old fashioned style of clothing seen in the antebellum era of flouncy petticoats. Except for her attire, the woman looked perfectly natural and it did not occur to Mrs Saunders that the figure was not human. Yet as she drew near, as near even as to outstretch her hand in greeting, the lady disappeared.

On reflection Mrs Saunders considered that this vision must have been a kind of material corroboration of the voice she had heard earlier in her drawing room.

When Mr Saunders listened to this account from his wife, he was inclined to be sceptical. Hearing clanks and taps in the basement was one thing, seeing apparitions of smiling southern belles was quite another. Yet, a few days later Mr Saunders was looking for something in the basement when he was taken aback by the sudden appearance of a woman that fitted the description his wife had given of her vision, sitting on a trunk. Likewise, as he cautiously moved towards the figure, it vanished. No further sighting was had, but now the Saunders'

listened and kept a look out in the hope of one day being graced with another visitation.

Drama at Tutbury Castle
The terrifying clawing

Tutbury Castle in Staffordshire is known for being the prison in which Mary Queen of Scots was held in the 16th century for many years prior to her execution in London. Her ghost is reputed to haunt the castle and its grounds. Typically dressed in a black gown, the doomed queen has been seen drifting across the wide lawn that graces the front of this part-ruined, part-inhabited

Tutbury Castle

Norman castle.

But more recently the castle has been the focus of a gathering of ghost hunters who descended on the place to try to capture some evidence of spectral activity. In 2003, on Walpurgis Night – springtime equivalent of Halloween – a large number of enthusiasts from across the country took part in what was publicised as the 'World's Biggest Ghost Hunt'. Many such assemblies take place in modern times, and usually nothing of any note occurs. But on this occasion, even the sceptics were surprised at what happened.

The most haunted part of the castle is the King's Chamber, where Charles I took refuge from the Roundheads during the English Civil War. The spectral activity reported to occur in this room has been so frequent, and so aggressive, that the room had to close to the public. Visitors were said to be touched, shoved, even slapped by unseen forces; others said they felt a cold breeze.

Hence a special visit was arranged on Walpurgis Night when the potential for ghostly appearance traditionally peaks.

A storm was building in the sky above the rolling Staffordshire countryside - and the atmosphere was just right for a frightening night. Accompanying the group was a writer for the Derby *Evening Telegraph*, David Clensy. His account is interesting:

A walk through across the dimly lit main hall led to the chamber's unexceptional white door. Strange things started to happen to my brain as soon as I walked in there. Like many of the other visitors, I felt a little dizzy – almost queasy. But there were many possible reasons for this – the room was dimly lit, and strangely shaped – with a cone-like ceiling leading up to a skylight. The floor was sickeningly uneven, and carpeted with a migraine-inducing rug. And, most significantly, the temperature dropped dramatically from the oppressive main hall. So I took a deep breath and concentrated on rational thoughts. But like everyone in the room, the nerves were certainly welling up as Lesley gave a warning about the seriousness of what could happen once the lights were switched off. I shivered. The lights were flicked, and all was darkness. "Put your hand out in front of you," Lesley said. "Do you feel an icy wind?" I did, but I would need more than a draught to convince me. A woman in her 20s on the other side of the room gave a sudden shriek. "I've got the most terrible headache," she announced dramatically as Lesley put the lights back on and led her from the room.

Then Clensy went on to explain the most terrifying incident of the evening:

The bulky 6ft 2ins figure of Glenn Baggaley (26), of Derby, ran out of the King's Chamber, clearly shaken. 'It was horrible,' he said. 'I was stood in the room, and I suddenly felt an ominous presence. Then I felt a tapping on my right shoulder. I tried to keep calm, but then I felt a burning sensation in my neck. It was painful – like bad sunburn. Lesley turned the lights back on straight away, and discovered this,' Glenn pulled his collar down to reveal a long three-pronged claw mark on his neck, still oozing blood. Glenn is a bouncer in Derby city centre. He said he felt powerless and vulnerable. 'I don't mind admitting that I burst into tears,' he said. 'It was terrifying. I know it sounds daft for a bouncer to be so afraid.'

Fortunately a team of paramedics were on hand in case of any incident and were able to treat this man, as well as those who had fainted.

It might also be mentioned as an afterthought that on March 3, 1993, one Brenda Ray took some photographs of the main street through Tutbury with the castle ruins in the background. When the film was developed, one of the shots clearly shows an individual enrobed to the ground in a black cape walking down the middle of the road. A photograph of precisely the same location taken a moment later shows no such figure. Unless this is a spoof, how is it to be explained?

WALPURGIS NIGHT

Throughout Europe on the night of April 30, it is said ghosts, witches and evil spirits are released into the air. The night is a sort of springtime equivalent of Halloween. The roots of the custom lay in a pagan festival celebrating the beginning of summer (May 1). It later became associated with the Anglo-Saxon nun St Walburga, a healer with miraculous medicines, who travelled to Germany

as a missionary in the eighth century.
After her death she acquired a
reputation as a spiritual protector
against black magic, and when her
Roman Catholic feast day was made
May 1, her skills were naturally
called upon to combat the sinister
phantoms abroad on this night.

The Poltergeist of Calvados Castle
Four months of hell

A relatively modern chateau in Normandy seems an unlikely place of haunting but for several months in 1875/6 it became the focus of at times violent poltergeist activity. To this day no explanation has been given for the disturbances which therefore remain a mystery. All we know is that the chateau was built on the site of a ruined Norman castle which was said to be haunted.

The inhabitants of the chateau have wished to remain anonymous and so they are not identified in the following account.

The first strange noises were heard just after midnight on October 12, 1875. The next morning, the owner endeavoured to find out their cause, thinking it most likely to be local miscreants. He had just summoned the gardener, Auguste, and the coachman, Emile, to help him when his large dogs started barking at some woods in the grounds.

Thinking they may have sniffed out last night's perpetrators, he expected any moment to see the trespassers emerge with hands raised in surrender. Instead, the dogs' fury turned to whimpers and they ran out of the woods with their tails between their legs. The three men went to investigate with pistols cocked at their side, yet found no trace of anyone.

This marked the beginning of a series of inexplicable events that became more and more frightening. The following evening, Abbe Y, tutor to the owner's son Maurice, came downstairs slightly embarrassed at the ridiculousness of what he was going to announce, namely that his armchair had suddenly shifted of its own accord. He was sure he saw it move out of the corner of his eye.

Already unnerved by the experience in the garden, the owner

took what the tutor said seriously. He went with him to his room. To test for further activity, he stuck a piece of gummed paper to the floor beside the leg of the armchair and told Abbe Y to ring for him if anything untoward happened again.

Sure enough, later that evening, the owner heard a frantic ringing on the bell and hurryied up to the tutor's room. There he saw Abbe Y in his bed with a sheet pulled up to his nose shuddering with fear. The armchair had indeed moved about a metre, several candlesticks and statuettes lay on the floor, which Abbe Y claimed had simply fallen by themselves, and he had heard a loud rapping on the bedroom wall too. The owner's daughter had heard the rapping and was frightened as well.

Noises continued on subsequent nights in different parts of the chateau, as though whatever was causing them was able to move from one place to another. Sometimes the noises were extraordinarily loud – thunderous blows, and thumps on the stairs, as though a great steel ball was bouncing down them.

Each time, the owner would arm

himself and his servants with firearms and bravely investigate. Yet each time, they found nothing. At a loss at what to do or who to turn to for help, the perplexed owner tried the local priest, who promptly declared the activity to be supernatural, and there was nothing to be done.

So far, the ghost – for all now agreed there must surely be a ghost – had restricted itself to noises, albeit very loud ones.

But one stormy night in November, the entity demonstrated a voice, of sorts. Above the howling wind a distinct shriek was heard. Everyone assumed there must be a woman in distress outside. Yet when they stood at the window to try to see her, the sound seemed to come from inside the chateau.

The family kept close together in the drawing room, then moans were heard from the staircase. The men of the house investigated, yet as before there was nothing. More noises associated with distress occurred on subsequent evenings – sobs and panting turned into howling shrieks, as though a woman was in deep suffering.

Army officer visits

A friend of the family who had been told about all this ghostly activity, decided this was too much to resist and came to stay for a while to see for himself. Though a sceptical army officer, he did keep a revolver by his bedside just in case. Shortly after falling asleep in the empty green room from where many of the noises seemed to come, the guest was awoken by a soft rustling sound, like fabric brushing past, close to his bed. Something started tugging at his blankets. The officer sat up and in a loud majorly voice demanded to know who was there. Hearing nothing, he attempted to light a candle, but each time it blew out. Meanwhile, his blankets continued to be pulled from his bed, like a childish joke. When the officer cocked his gun and threatened to shoot if the presence did not declare itself, a violent tug of the bedclothes removed them completely. He pulled the trigger, firing his gun three times. That seemed to quieten the activity. The officer was left alone for the rest of the night. On inspection the next morning, he found three bullet holes in the wall but little other evidence of his disturbed night.

When another priest was sent by the bishop to Calvados Castle to investigate, the noises disappeared from the moment he stepped through the door. As soon as the priest left, they returned. Indeed, with a vengeance, it seemed. Noises became even louder, and now attacked Maurice's room, hammering on the door. A priest was called again, and this time attempted an exorcism in January 1876. This marked the beginning of the end of the family's ordeal. The haunting had come to centre on the boy's room. On one particular night during a series of exorcism rites, the cry of a man rose up, as though emitting a final volley of rage, accompanied by pounding on the door of the green room. This was followed by a cough and splutter as if suffering the throes of death. And after that night, all fell quiet for some considerable time. The following autumn some sounds were heard again but not on anything like the scale of this prolonged period of disturbance. The whole saga was recorded and published as a book in

1893, *Annales des Sciences Psychiques*, by one M J Morice.

Apparitions at Versailles
Edwardian ladies glimpse the past

When two academic ladies took a wrong turning while walking through the gardens of Versailles in 1901, their world view was to be changed forever. Whatever one or the other Edwardian tourist saw would challenge their traditional beliefs so powerfully that the two women felt compelled to publish an account of their experience, entitled *An Adventure*.

Both were daughters of Anglican clergymen. Annie Moberly, 55, was daughter to the Bishop of Salisbury and head of St Hugh's College, Oxford University. Eleanor Jourdain,

Versailles

35, was due to begin a post there as her assistant. To get to know each other better the two women decided to take a summer vacation together in Paris, where Ms Jourdain had an apartment.

After seeing the palace at Versailles, they decided to visit the Petit Trianon, a small chateau built in the grounds by Louis XVI as a private retreat for his queen Marie Antoinette. Somehow they seemed to lose their way after missing a turning, and found themselves walking down a quiet lane. From now onwards, several curious things happened, some of which the two women appeared to disagree on when comparing notes later. In this lane there was a domestic servant leaning out of a window shaking a bed sheet. It turns out that Ms Jourdain had no recollection whatsoever of this person, and Ms Moberley remembered it as clear as day: it happened right beside them as they passed.

What the women did agree on was the distinct change of atmosphere here, now quite oppressive and melancholy. Ms Jourdain later wrote, 'Everything suddenly looked

Petit Trianon

unnatural, therefore unpleasant; even the trees seemed to become flat and lifeless, like wood worked in tapestry. There were no effects of light and shade, and no wind stirred the trees.' Ms Moberley said she felt she was walking in a dream.

When they came to where the lane divided into three paths, they encountered two men dressed in 18th century attire: smart grey-green costumes with three-cornered hats, as though in fancy dress. One of them offered directions but in an offhand manner difficult to understand.

They came to a bridge with a kiosk beside it. There sat a rough, sinister-looking man wearing a cocked hat and cloak. Both women felt quite ill at ease. They remarked that he slowly turned his gaze to them, revealing a face severely marked by smallpox. After crossing the bridge and at last coming into the gardens in front of the Petit Trianon, Ms Moberley saw a lady sitting on the grass sketching, again dressed in 18th century clothes. Yet Ms Jourdain saw no one.

The two women did not discuss the afternoon until about a week later, and only then did they realise they were each deeply affected by what had happened, yet their accounts differed in detail on account of their individual experiences.

They decided to re-visit Versailles separately to see if these apparitions, as they both believed them to be, were a 'one-off' or not. Curiously, on subsequent visits, neither was able to find the lane they had walked along, not the kiosk nor bridge where the unpleasant man had sat.

The two ladies each arrived at the same radical conclusion which caused considerable stir when they came to publish their story. Not only did they claim that the Trianon was haunted, they even suggested they had become caught in a 'time slip', and had actually travelled back to the time of the French Revolution in the 1790s. Moberley was convinced that the woman sketching on the grass had actually been Marie Antoinette herself.

Their book, published under the pseudonyms Elizabeth Morison and Frances Lamont, drew howls of derision from sceptics. A biography about a French aristocrat and poet

Philippe de Montesquiou maintained that he lived nearby at the time of Moberley's and Jourdain's visit to Versailles, and had a penchant for throwing fancy dress parties. As part of the entertainment, dramatic sketches in period costume were performed for the guests. It is thought the two women had simply stumbled upon a rehearsal for one of these performances, though this would not explain the eerie atmosphere they had encountered.

TIME TRAVEL

Many psychics believe it possible to travel, psychically, to a different land in the past. With the use of mind-control exercises such as meditation, lucid dreaming, and out-of-body experiences, subjects can be transported psychologically to their own past lives and those of others from different periods of history. States of precognition (looking into the future) and retrocognition (seeing the past) are believed to allow the subject brief glimpses of actual events. Albert Einstein's theory of relativity proved that within the laws of physics it is possible to go forwards in time, though no law yet exists to show travel backwards in time.

Albert Einstein

Holy Cross church. The factory workers finish their shift at 4am and on several occasions after leaving the premises they have noticed a hooded monk cross the road and vanish among the gravestones in the churchyard.

The monk is described as wearing a red cowl, with a white face and surly expression. Some say he is transparent, and others that his feet do not appear to touch the ground and that he floats along.

One of the factory women reported one occasion when riding her bicycle along the road past the church seeing the ghost cross directly in front of her. It was so close she did not have time to brake and rode through the phantom mist. She felt nothing other than a cold dampness.

Nothing is known for certain about the identity of the red monk, but a local tradition says that two rectors of this church were expelled during the Reformation and that this figure represents one of them.

CHURCH, ABBEY AND CEMETERY

Phantom Monk of Holy Cross
The witness of night shift workers in Basildon

Several women who work a night shift at a factory in Basildon, Essex, claim to have seen a phantom monk in the nearby churchyard of

The Madonna of Bachelor's Grove
Chicago's most haunted site

Bachelor's Grove Cemetery

L ying just outside the Chicago suburb of Midlothian is one of the city's most haunted places. Bachelor's Grove is a cemetery where literally hundreds of paranormal phenomena have been reported over the years. The name probably comes from the multitude of unmarried German labourers who migrated here to help build the Illinois-Michigan Canal in the mid-nineteenth century.

The last burial to take place in this one-acre cemetery was in 1989, largely because the numerous hauntings reported in the 1970s and '80s put people off.

The most common sights are of elusive coloured lights at night. Even stranger are the sightings of magical animals and weird sounds, some of which have been recorded.

One recurring image is of a floating house in the distance. From a gravel path visitors on separate occasions have described the same house which does not exist in daylight. It is white with two porch pillars, a lamp illuminated in the window and a swing. But the house is never said to be in the same place. As witnesses approach it, the image reduces and vanishes.

The most famous ghost of Bachelor's Grove is the Madonna. She tends to be seen when there is a full moon, walking about the cemetery cradling a baby in her arms. The ghost is supposed to relate to a woman who is buried there next to her baby son.

A famous photograph of the Madonna of Bachelor Grove was taken during an investigation of the site in August 1991. Behind a tree in the foreground is the distinct image of a long-haired woman in a white robe sitting on a tombstone with her hands in her lap. She has an almost translucent quality. Professional photographers have ruled out any double exposure. According to the photgrapher, Mari Huff of the Ghost Research Society, this woman was not visible at the time the picture was taken.

PHANTOM MONKS AND NUNS

Many religious sites are believed to be haunted by monks and nuns. Abbeys, monasteries and nunneries, where they used to live and may have suffered martyrdom, have accounts of phantom appearances. The Reformation in Britain produced its fair share of atrocities. The abbess of Holy Trinity Church in York, for example, was murdered by Henry VIII's soldiers when she tried to bar their entry. As she lay dying she vowed to return to haunt the building and has been seen at various times since. Cloisters at Canterbury Cathedral are said to be haunted by a hooded monk. However, not all hauntings are the result of bad experiences. Some spirits return to a place beloved during their time on earth, especially if the monk or nun spent virtually all their life there.

Mystery Force on Baltic Island
Terrified horses and displaced coffins

The island of Oesel, offshore of Estonia in the Baltic Sea, was an untroubled land of Teutonic fiefdoms for several centuries before the Republic of Estonia expropriated the estates early in the 20th century. An ecclesiastical court used to convene regularly to hear any local grievances. In 1844 a strange complaint was put to them by several people whose horses had been deeply disturbed by strange noises issuing from the private chapel of Arensburg cemetery.

One of the horse owners described how she had tethered her horse near the Buxhoewden family chapel in order to pay respects to her mother's grave. But within a few minutes the animal began to neigh dreadfully, clearly upset by something. It soon collapsed and frothed at the mouth. The woman ran to find a vet, who only just managed to save the beast's life, by bleeding it.

The following Sunday, several people tied their horses to the same point outside the Buxhoewden chapel and a similar experience was recorded. Each horse appeared to tremble violently as though in terror. Some witnesses at the time claimed to hear strange groans coming from inside the chapel, yet no one was there.

The ecclesiastical court was at a loss for an explanation. When the same thing happened the following week, and this time four horses died, the court officials suggested perhaps something poisonous was on the ground and that for the time being horses should be tethered elsewhere until the matter is cleared up.

Funeral at the chapel

Then, some time afterwards, a funeral was held at the Buxhoewden chapel, with some alarming occurrences. When the service was under way, mourners heard noises coming up from the crypt below, a sort of groaning, as described by witnesses previously. At the end of the funeral, when the officials in charge went down below to make a place for interment, they were aghast to see most of the coffins belonging to the Buxhoewden family had been disinterred and lay in a muddle.

Outraged that such an act of desecration should have happened, the head of the family, Baron de Guldenstubbe, personally investigated the matter. Having replaced the coffins, he and colleagues were bemused to find, on returning another day, that once again they had been removed from their rightful places. The baron had instructed men to inspect the entire vault to look for signs of wrongful entry, even sections of the floor were exposed. Yet no evidence of mischief could be found.

The only solution, he decided, was to maintain a round-the-clock vigilance for three days and then re-inspect. Ashes were spread about the floor of the vault and steps down to the heavy entrance door so that any footfall would show.

After the three days were up, an inspection committee arrived and noted no disturbance of the ashes leading to the entrance. They opened the door and to their amazement, one and all, the family coffins were again in a state of disarray. One, belonging to a suicide, was even standing on its end with the lid ajar.

No explanation was ever found for these disturbances. An official report was submitted by Baron de Guldenstubbe but nothing is known of any further strange activity.

Invisible Monk at Michelham Priory
Photographic evidence of a ghost?

On the evening of Saturday 5 April 2003 members of the Ghost Club assembled at Michelham Priory in Sussex to carry out an all night investigation in the belief that the place is haunted. They moved about the priory with camcorders and various monitoring equipment.

Certain cold areas were noted and some members felt quite scared, even unwell, in some rooms. But it was the Prior's Chamber where the most startling phenomena would be revealed. A strange creaking was heard near a window enticing the team to gather in the room. Unfortunately the camcorder suddenly seemed to malfunction, so the leading investigator, Kathy Gearing, took a number of shots with her digital

Michelham

Charles Dickens   *Siegfried Sassoon*   *Julian Huxley*   *Edith Sitwell*

camera. When she examined them later, an extraordinary vision emerged. Although her flash had failed, one photograph, though dark, clearly shows a man apparently sitting in a chair by the window. Kathy swears no one was in such a position when she took the shot. She immediately sent the picture to her expert colleague, Philip Carr, for enhancement, after which the figure could be seen dressed in black with longish hair and a beard, and in fact standing not sitting. On examining her camera, Kathy found it to work perfectly. Indeed this photo was the only one with no flash. There appears to be no explanation for the appearance of this figure which no one actually saw at the time of the investigation.

THE GHOST CLUB

One of the oldest surviving organizations associated with paranormal research is the Ghost Club of London. A number of Cambridge University fellows set up the club in 1862 to share ideas about the nature of ghosts and psychic phenomena. As much of their purpose was to expose fakes as to affirm authentic experiences. With the demise of the initial generation the club faded but revived intermittently, usually when an acolyte took up the cause. Among prominent members were Charles Dickens, Julian Huxley, Siegfried Sassoon, Earl Mountbatten and Edith Sitwell. Since 1993 membership has been open to anyone seriously interested in exploring the immense realm of the paranormal.

HOTELS, INNS AND RESTAURANTS

Godfather's Pizza in Utah
Research team capture evidence of ghost

A pizza restaurant in Ogden, Utah, has been the subject of extensive psychical investigation since a series of unaccountable events prompted the owner to call in the Utah Paranormal Exploration and Research team (UPER) in 1999. They came with plenty of equipment – video and digital cameras, and hyper-sensitive audio recording devices.

They also did their research on the place to find out if there was any useful background. It turns out that before the restaurant was built the land may have been a paupers' field (where the poor were buried) and Ogden City Cemetery lay further down the hill. The first strange phenomena to disturb the restaurant owners were some bizarre electrical occurrences. It all started one night when the jukebox, which was switched off at the time, started playing music. Later some fluorescent

Phantom boy at Godfather's Pizza?

lights shot out of their sockets and whizzed across the room. Unusual noises were heard, such as whistling in the kitchen when no one was there. Even ghostly figures were observed drifting about, in particular two young boys. The owner said one of them actually walked right through him before disappearing into a wall.

The most interesting experience at Godfather's to be recorded by UPER happened in 2000. After the restaurant had shut for the day, a sort of mist appeared in the middle of the dining room. The manifestation only lasted a few seconds but long enough for UPER to catch it on film. The photograph revealed a boy, or at least a short person. The owner said the apparition seemed like one of the boys in the mist that he had seen earlier in the restaurant. The boy, whose face is in profile, is wearing a billowy shirt and stiff white collar. Otherwise, the features are too blurred to bear description, yet the whole is unmistakably the figure of a small person.

Florrie of the Red Lion
Sinister haunting of Avebury

One of the most haunted pubs in the South West of England is the Red Lion Inn at Avebury in Wiltshire. The pub is situated within one of the ancient stone circles here, which together constitute the largest prehistoric monument in Europe. Before the Red Lion became a pub, it was a 17th century farmhouse. The building was erected around a dependable well from which water could be drawn for everyday use.

One of its earliest inhabitants was believed to be murdered here after some outlaws he had locked up in his cellar tricked him and then stabbed him to death. His ghost is said to haunt the place and has been seen carrying a knife.

Early in the 19th century the house acquired a licence and became a coaching inn. Some staff at the inn have reported hearing a ghostly clatter of hooves on courtyard stones, others claim even to have spotted a horse-drawn carriage coming into the yard.

The best-known ghost of the Red

Lion is Florrie, the wife of a soldier who lived here during the English Civil War. While he was away on military duty, she took a lover. When her husband returned to find them together, he flew into a rage, shot the lover and stabbed his wife to death. He is said to have disposed of the body by throwing her down the well situated in the middle of what is now the pub. Her ghost has been seen drifting about the bar area, issuing up and down the well which is covered over now by glass. Her presence is associated with inexplicable mists that sometimes arise in the pub and have been caught on camera by investigating psychic researchers.

Guests at the inn have sometimes complained of feeling strangely cold at night even in summer, others have been so disturbed by a presence in the inn that they have left during the night.

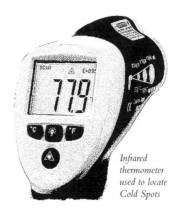

Infrared thermometer used to locate Cold Spots

COLD SPOTS

Sometimes areas of distinct coldness, known as cold spots, can accompany haunting activity. Some researchers believe they are caused by a vortex, through which a ghost will travel to reach another realm. Witnesses may feel a sudden rush of cold air, as though a door had been opened on a cold day, or simply a mass of icy air within a room or passage. The change of temperature is associated with the manifestation of a ghost. The theory is that because a ghost has no body heat of its own, it draws heat, or energy, from its surroundings in order to materialise. Ghosts are believed to be capable of drawing energy from sensitive people who might suddenly feel cold as a result. Even tiny changes in body temperature can affect a person's physiology and induce a fear response.

Postechaise Hotel of County Durham
Restless soul in Bishop Auckland

The following modern experience of ghosts in a hotel in County Durham was recorded by a clairvoyant and astrologer, Jan Jordan. At the time of her visit, the hotel was hosting a psychic fair. The original part of the hotel dates back to the 18th century when it was a coach house, now the public bar, still with its low old beams, bench seats and fireplace. A newer wing had been added since then consisting of a restaurant and function room. And it was here, down a long corridor towards the function room that Ms Jordan first saw an old-fashioned looking gentleman dressed in a top hat and tails, briefly before he/it disappeared.

As Ms Jordan approached the function room, the space seemed to 'swirl', she said, and then as she looked further she saw not a room but an open cobbled courtyard with carriages entering through an archway. Once again she saw the man in the top hat. Making enquiries later, it turns out the function room used to be the old courtyard. Ms Jordan believes she had glimpsed the past through a time slip.

Her experience overnight at the hotel was even more interesting. She awoke to hear a voice speaking close to her bed, as well as what sounded like rustling skirts. Then through the gloom, Ms Jordan picked out the outline of a figure in the room, a young woman, quite thin with pale face and dark hair. The clairvoyant understood that this girl had been brought here against her will to be married to a man she hated. Rather than go through with this arranged marriage she committed suicide and ever since was a restless soul.

On making enquiries once again, the hotel staff admitted that the room she slept in had a reputation for 'paranormal activity' from time to time. A young woman fitting the description of the apparition witnessed by Ms Jordan had been reported before, appearing on the stairs and landing, as had the gentleman in the top hat.

THE WORKPLACE

The White House
Perennial Abraham Lincoln

The workplace and residence of the US president, based in Washington, is believed to be haunted by several ghosts. Built in 1800, it was first occupied by President John Adams, and has six residential storeys and more than 130 rooms.

The oldest known phantom is that of the original First Lady, Abigail Adams, who has been seen carrying laundry to the East Room before vanishing through walls. The later president Andrew Jackson's laughter and swearing is said to be heard sometimes coming from the Rose Room, where he was fond of sleeping. The first president to die while in office is believed to have raised a spectre in the attic.

However, the most illustrious – and interesting – of the ghosts to haunt the White House is that of Abraham Lincoln, the 16th president. He himself had a premonition of his death. He informed an advisor shortly

Abigail Adams

before his assassination in 1865 that he had woken up in the night to hear the sound of weeping: 'I wandered downstairs until I came to the East Room. Before me was a catafalque with a corpse whose face was covered. "Who is dead?" I demanded of the mourners. "The President," was the reply. "He was killed by an assassin."'

Lincoln's murder at the end of the American Civil War by a Confederate sympathiser, John Wilkes Booth, seems to have generated a persistent presence of the man. A phantom appearance has been spotted in various places, inside and outside the White House. Theodore Roosevelt admits seeing the ghost of Abraham Lincoln prowling about: 'I think of Lincoln, shambling, homely, with his sad, strong, deeply furrowed face. I see him in different rooms and halls.'

Staff claim to have seen him putting on his boots in the Lincoln bedroom, and others have reported hearing a knocking on bedroom doors at night, some actually seeing an apparition of the former president. Indeed while Winston Churchill was staying in the Lincoln bedroom during the Second World War, admittedly under considerable strain at the time, he saw the ghost of Lincoln and promptly asked to be moved to a different room.

The Haunting of Coutts
Sensational release of Elizabethan duke

One of the most prestigious banks in England is Coutts, also known as the Queen's bank because

The White House

its most illustrious client is Queen Elizabeth II. Founded in 1692, the bank has always had a prosperous clientele who expect comfortable surroundings on visiting. But in 1992 several employees at the headquarters in the Strand complained of strange things occurring. Lights and computers started to flicker erratically and a black silhouette was seen ghosting through the offices, sometimes apparently with no head. When employees became too scared to come into work, the bank knew they had to do something. The nature of the problem was beyond the call of their regular maintenance consultants, so the bank took the unprecedented step of commissioning the College of Psychic Studies to investigate. The college sent their psychic medium Eddie Burks, a civil engineer by profession, who had discovered his gift for spiritual healing in 1975. His extraordinary results caused an international sensation.

Burks surveyed the premises and interviewed employees, then held a séance to see if he could contact the spirit that seemed to be haunting the place. He duly managed to contact a ghost whom a priest and historian later identified as a wealthy aristocrat from the Elizabethan period, the 4th duke of Norfolk, Thomas Howard. He was executed in 1572 for plotting to marry Mary, Queen of Scots, and depose the reigning monarch Elizabeth I.

Although the execution took place well before Coutts was even founded, it happened nearby, and it is thought that the duke's spirit had somehow become 'trapped' within the bank's premises on the Strand.

The execution had left the spirit irate and bitter. Indeed it pleaded with Burks to be released from its torment. Burks agreed to try, and managed to call up the dead man's daughter. Her figure appeared dressed in radiant white light and took hold of her father's hand and led him away. The two gradually disappeared into the light.

On 12 January of the following year the spirit again contacted Burks and apparently thanked him for rescuing him, for he was now in peace with his daughter.

Boots Go Marching
At the army surplus store

When Mr A M Sharp took ownership of an army surplus store in the spring of 1952, he acquired more than simply the stock of military accoutrements that came with the sale. His predecessor had warned Mr Sharp of hearing strange noises on the premises, particularly upstairs, and sometimes quite deafening bangs. Knowing him to be a veteran of the First World War who suffered a good deal on the battlefield, Mr Sharp thought it must be a case of bad nerves playing tricks on his mind, and thought little more of it.

However, when the new owner was working late one night he too began to hear one of the noises that had been described: the regular tread of boots on the floor above. Knowing no one to be upstairs, Mr Sharp checked outside to see if anyone was next door, but that shop was clearly shut up for the night. He returned and decided to go upstairs and see for himself, admittedly now with some trepidation.

Half way up, the shopkeeper suddenly froze as he thought he saw – or rather sensed – a figure moving about on the landing. After a few minutes of remaining motionless, the figure, or whatever it was, seemed to have gone. No more disturbances happened that night and Mr Sharp locked up and went home, albeit in a somewhat nervous and perplexed state of mind.

This would not be the end of it. The next day, when Mr Sharp opened up his store, he discovered that several rows of army boots, which had been neatly stacked on shelves the previous day, were now scattered about the floor. His first thought was burglary. Yet on checking the doors and windows and any other possible point of entry all was as it should be: there was no sign of forced entry. Trying hard to stay calm and rational, the shopkeeper had to conclude that being flustered by these strange events he must have failed to lock the back door, and as a result intruders had come in. This evening he would make absolutely sure all was locked up before leaving the premises.

However, when he arrived the

next morning to see that the very same thing had happened again, Mr Sharp suddenly felt weak at the knees and had to sit down, completely at a loss for an explanation. Now he was forced to concede there might be a connection between the boots in disarray and the noise of footfall upstairs. Yet what could he do?

Then one evening while working late on some bookkeeping, Mr Sharp suddenly felt a hand on his shoulder. He quickly turned round, but no one was there. He heard the sound of retreating footsteps, yet there was no sign of anyone in the shop after that.

Hacks on the case

Gossip soon reached the ears of local newspaper editors. Reporters from the Lancashire *Evening Post* asked if they might visit the shop and perhaps stay a while to see if they too could experience these strange phenomena. So a vigil was kept one night. Before they settled down, the journalists checked upstairs for loose floorboards, window latches, and so on. Mr Sharp was ironically pleased to note that they too heard the sounds of heavy thumps upstairs. They also heard the

scrape of metal and what sounded like a chain being dragged across floorboards. On inspection a long chain was found in the corner of one otherwise empty room, yet Mr Sharp claimed no chain ever existed in his building.

Still feeling that somehow a practical joke must be the answer, the shopkeeper was sufficiently dismayed at finding the disarray of his shop each morning that he decided to call in a local clairvoyant, Frank Spencer. This specialist acknowledged the presence of more than one spirit entity inhabiting the premises. He said each of them was suffering in their plight of being 'tied' to the earth zone. Apparently the store had been built on the site of a former jail, and indeed the present cellar may once have been a medieval prison. It seems that Spencer's visit may have made a difference, for after a few weeks the disturbances ceased, and Mr Sharp was left to conduct his business in peace.

Terror in Alcatraz
San Francisco's Haunted Prison

An island in San Francisco Bay was once charmingly known as The Island of the Pelicans. That was before it was taken over by the US army in 1912 and used as a fort and prison. Native Americans say the island was always a sinister place, an abode of evil spirits. When it subsequently turned into a state penitentiary, one of the highest security prisons in the country, reports began to seep out of horrible occurrences in the cells, of such terrifying intensity that some inmates did not survive.

One particularly nasty cell was known as the 'hole', a windowless D Block dungeon where red-eyed demons were said to terrorise its occupants. One night in the 1940s an inmate, knowing what awaited him, was dragged screaming into the cell. Terrible yells were heard all night.

By morning he was dead. An autopsy showed beastlike claw marks to his neck which were certified as non-suicidal.

Other prisoners have tried to break out of the escape-proof fortress but have paid with their lives. Others have been murdered, still others, unable to bear the torment, have committed suicide. The prison's most famous inmate, 'Scarface' Al Capone, reputedly spent his time calmly sitting on his bunk playing tunes on the banjo.

Known as the Rock, Alcatraz closed as a working prison in 1963 and is now open to tourists. Many claim to feel the fear and panic of past inmates as they wander about the menacing corridors and cells. Some claim to hear phantom footsteps and even the screams of prisoners being beaten. Others say they feel as though they are being watched and wish to leave sooner than they expected.

Alcatraz

BAD ENERGY

Parapsychologists say that in a place such as Alcatraz where so much trauma has been experienced, a degree of negative energy can remain within the building. Even though all suffering ceased in 1963, the place can feel like a huge haunted house.

WAR ZONE

HAUNTED BATTLEFIELDS

Traumatic events can sometimes lead to hauntings. For this reason battlefields are quite likely to be associated with spectral presence. The theory is that people who suffered violent death have somehow left behind an emotional residue which is trapped where the battle took place and might be perceived by individuals who are psychically attuned. Researchers say that 'fragments' of a battle can also become imprinted on the psychic space of the battleground and may become linked to a particular place, such as a rock, wood or river, where military conflict occurred. Professional re-enactors of battle scenes for public entertainment sometimes tell of hauntings they experience while in the field.

German Advance

Grand Apparitions at Edge Hill
Psychic impact of the Civil War

Some battle scenes produced such an impact – on the local people, the environment, say the atmosphere – that for months later crucial elements of the conflict were experienced by individuals as though the battles were being re-enacted.

One famous example is the Battle of Edge Hill in 1642, the first major clash of the English Civil War between the Royalist and Parliamentarian forces. More than 40,000 men engaged in this slaughter in which the fighting was so ferocious that peasants claimed to hear terrible echoes of the battle for weeks afterwards: the dread beat of the battle drum, musketfire, the clatter of arms, screams of soldiers dying in agony and their terrified chargers.

Exactly two months after the battle took place on 23 October, shepherds tending their flocks saw an immense apparition in the sky of military colours arrayed round them. For three hours the sounds of battle filled the air to the amazement of the onlookers. When they reported the phenomenon to the local judiciary, judges and townsfolk came out the next night, Christmas Day, and they too beheld this extraordinary spectacle: the two armies 'appeared in the same tumultuous warlike manner, fighting with as much spite and spleen as formerly'. Even Charles I, on receiving news of it, sent investigators to the scene and they saw the dreadful replay of their fellow infantrymen falling in battle, even recognising the faces of colleagues.

This phantom re-enactment caused such a commotion that a pamphlet describing the event was published. The title, in the verbose form typical of the day, ran as *The Prodigious Noises of War and Battle at Edge Hill, Near Keinton in Northamptonshire and its truth is certified by William Wood, Esq and the Justice of the Peace for the same County and Samuel Marshall, Preacher of God's word in Keinton and other persons of quality.*

Some investigators have claimed the noises can still be heard today, though not on anything like the grand scale experienced during that first Christmas after the battle.

CROMWELL'S GHOST RISES

The spectres of the two leaders of the Civil War, Charles I and Oliver Cromwell are said to have appeared again in history. The king was seen in the library at Windsor Castle where he is buried. Cromwell reappeared at his regional headquarters in Huntingdon and has been seen walking in Red Lion Square in London. But the leader of the Roundheads' most startling appearance came in 1832 when England was again in political turmoil, this time over the Reform Bill.

A violent mob attacked Apsley House, the London home of the Duke of Wellington. As the anxious soldier considered his options, the armoured figure of Cromwell rose before him, distinctly recognisable from portraits the duke had seen. No words issued from the phantom but a finger pointed to the angry crowd outside. Though nothing more happened the encounter proved decisive, for after the bill was passed Wellington told the story and admitted it had changed his mind in favour of reform.

Oliver Cromwell

Trauma of War-torn Gettysburg
Ghouls of the American Civil War

The American Civil War lasted as long as the First World War and cost over 600,000 lives. The most ferocious, sustained fighting the continent has ever seen happened in this most bloody of conflicts. One of the most decisive battles occurred at

Gettysburg in Pennsylvania, in 1863. The struggle lasted for three days, from July 1 to 3, ranging across the hills and woods as well as the little town itself. The fighting was intense and relentless, and resulted in 50,000 casualties and 5000 dead horses.

At strategic points on the terrain in and around Gettysburg there are said to be hauntings that echo and even re-enact passages of the battle. At Devil's Den, where Confederate snipers hid among the giant boulders to shoot at Unionists holding the key position of Little Round Top, there are many reports of figures in contemporary uniform brandishing arms. A group of tourists visiting the battleground were convinced they must have been viewing a re-enactment staged for their benefit when they saw soldiers in combat near the summit of Little Round Top, yet were aghast to learn from the ranger that there was no such performance.

Monument to the dead of Gettysburg

After the third day of battle when General Lee and surviving troops retreated back south, huge numbers of wounded Confederates remained behind. Farmhouses and barns were turned into improvised hospitals. Pennsylvania College and Daniel Lady Farm became two makeshift wards where hundreds of troops died in anguish. The horror suffered by General Ewell's corps is said still to haunt the farmhouses where the groans of the dying sometimes can be heard. One of the most haunted buildings of what was Pennsylvania College was the Hall, a stately columned structure with a cupola that served as a look-out for Lee and his staff. The building subsequently reverted to a college and students have since reported seeing soldiers pacing back and forth in the cupola and walking the corridor to it.

However, the main room used as a field ward bears the most gruesome legacy. While blood squirted over the walls as doctors did their best to operate, without anaesthetic, to save life and limb, the sheer volume of casualties meant many of the hopeless cases were left to die in agony. Many

received no burial either. The wails and moans of suffering have, some believe, left a residual echo within the masonry and can be picked up by those with psychic sensibilities.

About eight miles from Gettysburg the phantom of a Confederate soldier has been spotted at Cashtown Inn, a hostelry where the Southern army stayed on the eve of battle. At Hummelbaugh House, a residence in Gettysburg, the cries of Confederate Brigadier General William Barksdale are said to be audible on some nights. A witness of the general in his dying moments said he was repeatedly asking for water, and his unheeded requests continue to haunt the area. Even his faithful dog can be heard howling after his lost master.

CHILDREN OF ANTIETAM

Another battle ground of the Civil War to be haunted was Antietam near Sharpsburg in Maryland. The indecisive outcome nevertheless cost thousands of lives. Today the site looks much as it did in 1862. As with other horrific battlefields, hauntings in the form of gunfire and the smell

Battle of Antietam

of gunpowder have been reported. But what is different about Antietam is that a group of visiting children told their teacher that several of them heard a chanting, sounding like 'fa-la-la-la-la'. When the children repeated it, the teacher, who was a war buff, instantly recognised the tune as being the war cry of the Irish 69th New York corps, one of the Union forces. Their military anthem was Faugh a Ballach, or 'Clear the Way' in English. In Gaelic it is pronounced Fah-ah-bah-lah.

The teacher was convinced that the school children, who could not possibly have known this obscure military chant, had experienced a haunting of Antietam.

The Phantom Hun
Behind the lines in WWI

War-time strife presents many an opportunity for ghostly apparitions. The terror of battle and loss of life make for a traumatic setting. But one interesting story of the First World War happened behind the Western Front well away from the action.

Derelict farmhouses in deserted villages were prime sites for reserve munitions dumps. The Allied forces would choose strategically placed old buildings behind the front line to store arsenal for use as an emergency supply. One such site lay between

German spiked helmet of WWI

Laventie and Houplines near Bethune in France. Explosives were hidden in the cellar of an old farmhouse and soldiers were assigned to guard it, day and night. They had rations, fuel, reading material and a few games to wile away the long empty hours. They worked in shifts and conducted occasional reckies outside to check for anything unusual.

All was very uneventful, except, that is, on one occasion when there was a full moon. Then, the guard on duty heard what sounded like boot steps on cobbled stones. He rushed outside and some 20-30 metres away saw a figure. He challenged the figure and on receiving no reply fired two rounds of his rifle. Extraordinarily, the figure just vanished. An inspection the following morning revealed nothing out of place, no footprints or disturbance of any kind.

Nevertheless, the guards clearly suspected enemy infiltration and reported the matter to intelligence officers, who sent one of their members and a gendarme to join the guards. On the second night of the new vigil the intelligence officer, Edwin Woodhall (who later wrote up his account of the experience), was on duty and heard the same footsteps that had previously been reported. He woke the others. All quietly grabbed their guns and crept up the cellar stairs to peek out into the moonlight. There, not ten metres from their eyes, stood a figure dressed in a dark uniform. This time the figure moved to the side and then vanished as before. The guards searched the site for an hour or more but found no one.

The following night, however, a more distinct figure could be made out: this time a German uniform with spiked helmet was clearly visible, though it appeared to be smeared with earth. They watched at first in amazement as the figure knelt to the ground and turned over some bricks. Then they climbed out and challenged the man. As he turned around, however, the soldiers with their fingers at the trigger were terrified to see that his face was a mere skeleton. The skull nodded and the bricks dropped. The soldiers fired their rifles, three loud bangs piercing the still night air. As before, the phantom disappeared, never to be seen again.

More intelligence officers arrived and inspected. The munitions were moved to another location, and that was the end of strange happenings at Bethune.

But on researching the background to the area, Woodhall discovered the farmhouse had an interesting past. It had been occupied earlier in the war by German troops led by a sergeant major. The farmer had run away and left his young wife and infant. Feeling threatened by the German officer, the French woman fled to the village and stayed in the priest's house. An allied attack, meanwhile, forced the Germans to abandon their position.

According to witnesses, the sergeant major accused the farmer's wife of betraying them and shot both her and her child. He then turned on the priest who uttered these condemnatory last words as he lay dying: 'Evil man, your spirit will live on, and you will return when your hour comes to haunt this place until God sees fit to absolve your soul!'

Fleeing the bombing, the German was struck by shrapnel from an explosion and died on the cobbled road. The other Germans escaped.

The villagers buried everyone who died there, including the German sergeant major. His grave was situated close to the wall where the guards of the munitions dump had seen the phantom picking up bricks.

Private Challoner seen by Robert Graves
Poet glimpses walking dead

The extreme conditions of life in the trenches during the First World War took its toll in many ways. High levels of stress, fatigue and nervous disorder caused mental problems and hallucinations. Amid a plethora of accounts of perceived realms of the spirit, there appeared some multiple testimonies of the sighting of ghosts. The English poet Robert Graves gave the following account of his experience while in France during the war:

I saw a ghost at Bethune. He was a man called Private Challoner who had been at Lancaster with me and again in F Company at Wrexham. When he went out with a draft to join the First Battalion, he shook my hand and said: 'I'll meet you again in France, sir.' He was killed at Festburt in May and in June he passed by our C Company billet where we were just having a special dinner to celebrate our safe return from Cuinchy…

Challoner looked in at the window, saluted and passed on. There was no Royal Welsh battalion billeted within miles of Bethune at the time. I jumped up and looked out of the window, but saw nothing except a fag end smoking on the pavement. Ghosts were numerous in France at the time.

Strange Meeting
Apparition of Wilfred Owen

The well-known poet of the First World War, Wilfred Owen, is said to have appeared to his brother Harold in a trench dugout a short time after dying just a week before armistice. Harold was unaware of his brother's death when he experienced this strange but moving apparition.

I had gone down to my cabin thinking to write some letters. I drew aside the door curtain and stepped inside and to my amazement I saw Wilfred sitting in my chair. I felt shock run through me with appalling force and with it I could feel the blood draining away from my face. I did not rush towards him but walked jerkily into the cabin – all my limbs stiff and slow to respond. I did not sit down but looking at him I spoke quietly: 'Wilfred, how did you get here?' He did not rise and I saw that he was involuntarily immobile, but his eyes which had never left mine were alive with the familiar look of trying to make me understand; when I spoke his whole face broke into his sweetest and endearing dark smile. I felt no fear – I had not when I first drew my door curtain and saw him there; only exquisite mental pleasure at thus beholding him. All I was conscious of was a sensation of enormous shock and profound astonishment that he should be here in my cabin. I spoke again, 'Wilfred dear, how can you be here, it is just not possible…' But still he did not speak but only smiled his most gentle smile. This not speaking did not now as it had done at first seem strange or even unnatural; it was not only in some inexplicable way perfectly natural but radiated a quality which made his presence with me undeniably right and in no way out of the ordinary. I loved having him there: I could not and did not want to try to understand how he had got there. I was content to accept him, that he was here with me was sufficient. I could not question anything, the meeting in itself was complete and strangely perfect. He was in uniform and I remember thinking how out of place the khaki looked among the cabin furnishings. With this thought I must have turned my eyes away from him; when I looked back my cabin chair was empty…

Wilfred Owen

I felt the blood run slowly back to my face and looseness into my limbs and with these an overpowering sense of emptiness and absolute loss…I wondered if I had been dreaming but looking down I saw that I was still standing. Suddenly I felt terribly tired and moving to my bunk I lay down; instantly I went into a deep and oblivious sleep. When I woke up I knew with absolute certainty that Wilfred was dead.

Jungle Ghouls of Corregidor
Wartime menace in the Philippines

Soon after the Second World War began, the fight in the east became a desperate struggle for strategic advantage. The Philippine Islands was on the front line of fierce combat between Japan and the Western Allies. In one particularly brave endeavour a small detachment of American and Filipino marines made a last-ditch effort to prevent the Japanese army advancing across the jungle interior of the key island of Corregidor.

The only surviving inhabitants in the 1960s were some Filipino ex-soldiers and a contingent of firewood cutters. But according to local reports there were also the 'non-living', in fact they outnumbered the living. One reason the island remained so little populated was the widespread belief that the interior became haunted by ghosts of the past.

Terrified wood cutters returned from their expeditions into the jungle claiming to have seen figures dressed in war fatigues in a distraught state. They carried rifles, many stumbled as a result of severe wounds, and accompanying sounds of military effort, shouting and cries of pain were heard.

Even today marines on jungle exercises report coming face to face with phantom reconnaissance scouts who appear to represent figures dating to the same conflict.

Also reported is the phantom of a woman. Some claim she is red-haired and beautiful, others say they see her dressed in a Red Cross uniform clearly ministering to the sick and dying. The reports say she fades as twilight turns to dark and the witnesses are left surrounded by the groaning wounded.

Corregidor satellite view

OPEN SPACES

Fair at Avebury
Night time apparition among the stone circles

In October 1916 a woman by the name of Edith Olivier was driving on the road one evening from Devizes to Swindon in Wiltshire. It was dark and the rain was beginning to fall heavily. She turned off the road towards an inn where she might have a meal and stay the night.

As Edith squinted through the gloom great black megaliths appeared to the side of the road which she assumed, though never having visited Avebury before, must be part of the famous prehistoric stone circles that stand there. Looming massively out of the dark they created quite an impression. However, what was to follow was even more surprising.

Beyond the stones in a clearing there appeared to be a village fair taking place. All the sights and sounds you would associate with such an event of the time were suddenly visible. People happily wandered about with flaming torches, entertainers caused laughter with their daring acts of fire-eating, juggling, and the like. Yet curiously, none seemed perturbed by the weather. No one wore a raincoat or carried an umbrella. It was as though it wasn't raining at all, but instead a clement late-summer evening.

Edith drove on, keen to get to her destination to eat. Though puzzled, she simply assumed the event must be a local tradition.

Some years later Edith revisited Avebury, this time as part of a tour group. Remembering the curious fair, she asked her guide about it. He assured her that such an event did use to happen here but had died out long ago. In fact no fair had been staged since 1850. Furthermore there was no road to the place where she witnessed the proceedings – that had gone as well. The guide told her a dirt track did once go there but had long since fallen out of use and no longer existed.

What was Edith to make of all this? Had she become caught in a kind of time warp? For a brief spell, had she slipped back many decades to the Victorian era and somehow witnessed a phantom fair? The apparition remains a puzzle but Avebury has a reputation for mysterious sightings. Figures moving among the stones have been reported when no persons were there. Perhaps its location as a centre for ancient pagan rituals suggests the area holds some enigmatic power we have not yet fathomed.

Giant Green Man
Roadside spectre in Buckinghamshire

Modern sightings of a mysterious green man in various guises has prompted the conjecture that spirits are sometimes perceived in nature. Folklore about the Green Man goes back a long way. He was a kind of pagan fertility character that would appear in woodlands. Perhaps from this base motif sprang the medieval representation of him as a head with no body, half human and half tree, as depicted in church carvings on pillar and pew. Some pubs too, particularly in the Chiltern Hills, are named after him. Near one of these pubs, in

German 'green man' mask

Hughenden Valley, High Wycombe, Buckinghamshire, a curious incident occurred in September 1986.

Mark Nursey was driving home late at night, followed by his girlfriend behind him. As they passed Hughenden Crematorium on Cryers Hill a figure dressed in green suddenly appeared by the roadside in a frightening posture. Both Mark and his girlfriend Allyson saw it and were scared out of their wits. Mark described it: 'The most uncanny thing was the way it stood. It seemed to be wearing what I can only describe as a big green jumper. I couldn't make out the head or hands. It seemed to be stooping.'

When the incident appeared in the local newspaper, another witness, warehouseman Phil Mullett, came forward to say that he too had seen the green man in virtually the same spot:

It gave me quite a shock to read it. The account was so close to my own. It was about 9.30pm when I drove into Four Ashes Road and on turning my car lights on full I saw this green person appear from the right hand side of the road. It drifted out to the centre of the road and turned towards me. It waved its arms, not to frighten but as if to warn me to keep back. It drifted into the hedge on the other side of the road but as I got closer it came out again to the centre, turned and lifted its arms. I knew I was going to hit it. I think

I cried out or shouted something.

Phil braked and thought he must have hit the figure. But when he got out of his car there was no trace of him. He described the apparition as being about seven feet tall, was dressed in green but he couldn't remember seeing any legs or hands. The face seemed to have no features and was simply a grey orb.

The location was next to a forest which tradition says is haunted by a green man, hence the name of the local pub there. Perhaps also of interest about this location is its relation to a ley line that begins at one end of Four Ashes Road. As alignments of ancient sites believed to be endowed with mysterious power, such as stone circles and certain churches, ley lines offer an interesting extra dimension to the green man conundrum. The figure seen by Mark, Allyson and Phil appeared just metres away from the ley line.

'Too Tough To Die'
Ghost town in Arizona

The dusty streets of Tombstone, perhaps the most violent of the 19th century cowboy towns, was the scene of many a showdown. The most famous gunfight happened at the OK Corral, an old horse enclosure, where law enforcers confronted a cowboy gang in an alley nearby. The fight lasted 30 seconds and 30 bullets were fired. Surprisingly perhaps, only three died as a result, others were wounded. But repercussions through vendettas went on for the next six months.

The upshot is that these gunfights, of which the one at OK Corral is just one of many, produced their fair share of phantoms. The saloon of Tombstone, where some 26 killings happened, is said to be haunted by over 30 ghosts. The toughest gunfighters were also the hardest

Tombstone, 1891

drinkers. Their favourite haunt was the town's notorious Bird Cage Theatre, named after cribs suspended from the ceiling in which 'painted ladies' would swing on their perches. Below would be ranged the varied clientele: poker players, card dealers, barmen, drunks and cowboys out to do a dirty deal. Many a night would end in a shoot out – bullet holes still pepper the ceiling as testimony. Losers would end up buried on Boot Hill (so named because internees still wore their boots).

Large-scale fires in the 1880s ravaged much of the town and by the end of the decade it was virtually abandoned. Tombstone then literally became a 'ghost town'. Now a tourist venue, the town has been left much as it was in the 19th century. The only growth seen here since then is of ghost stories to unsettle nervous visitors.

One common spectre is of a stage assistant in Bird Cage Theatre who dresses in black striped trousers, sporting a car-dealer's visor. Carrying a clipboard that keeps a tally of the gambling, he appears from one end of the room, strolls across stage, where

lewd cabaret was once performed, and then vanishes. Some say that if you listen carefully you can still hear the faint echo of cowboy songs being played and singing and laughter. Others report the smells of cigar smoke and scent in the bedrooms.

Although ghost investigators to the town, now a national museum, have been unable to capture any ghouls on film, they do say that ghostly activity has registered on their electrical equipment. Small orbs of light have been recorded floating upwards from the floor. A face has been seen in a landscape painting. At Nellie Cashman's Restaurant, open to tourists, employees and customers have observed dishes crashing to the floor for no apparent reason. And beside Wells Fargo coach stop, drivers and passengers have been seen alighting from a phantom stagecoach before making their way into the Grand Hotel. Perhaps it is no surprise that Tombstone, once a hive of Wild West gunslingers, is nicknamed the 'Town Too Tough To Die'.

GHOST LIGHTS

Moving lights or orbs sometimes seen, even captured on film, in particular places are believed by are also known as spook lights, they are often believed to haunt open roads and cemeteries. The lights sometimes

Ghost Lights

many to represent the early stages of a manifestation of a spirit or ghost. They are usually described as spherical and lantern-like, and sometimes are only visible under infra-red light which is why they might be caught on camera but not observed by the naked eye. Ghost lights may react to sound and other light. Sometimes they have been known to react to observers, hence their association with the ghosts of past lives. In the USA, where they accompany an apparition, such as on the Isle of Skye in 1950 when a medical doctor reported seeing an orb of light precede the vision of a cloaked woman holding a baby. In Hessdalen in a remote region of Norway, unaccountable ghost lights appeared in the 1980s prompting a scientific monitoring programme, also filmed. Underground noises sometimes accompanied the lights as well, but no consensus was reached to explain the phenomenon.

Chants in the Bermuda Triangle
Return of the disappeared?

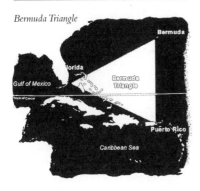

Bermuda Triangle

Reports of missing vessels and aircraft entering an area south of Bermuda in the Atlantic Ocean have spawned various theories of strange forces operating that have baffled scientists. The Bermuda Triangle, as it has become known, spans approximately between three landmarks: from Miami in Florida to Puerto Rico in the Caribbean, to Bermuda. The mysteries began in the 19th century. The first major disaster occurred in 1918 when the US supply ship *Cyclops* had set out from Barbados and vanished without issuing a single distress signal. No trace of the vessel or the 309 crew on board was ever found.

Perhaps the most famous air disappearance was Flight 19 of the US Navy. On December 5, 1945 a training exercise of five TBM Avenger bombers took off from Lauderdale Florida and flew eastwards out to sea. A scheduled flight path of more than 300 miles was due to bring them back to base, but they never returned. The weather was good throughout. The pilot in charge radioed to say they were on course but two hours later all contact had been lost.

A search plane was scrambled with 13 crew on board. That too never returned. To this day there is no explanation for what happened.

USS Cyclops *in Hudson Bay*

Grumman TBM Avenger bombers

Whilst these strange incidents in themselves apparently involve no ghostly activity, they provide an interesting background to other accounts of strange phenomena associated with the Bermuda Triangle.

Dr McCall's experience

This area is also called Devil's Triangle or the Hoodoo Sea by those who believe that the region is a haunt of tormented souls from the slave trade. Millions of negro slaves went overboard while in transit from West Africa to the West Indies and southern United States. Their spirits are said to be capable of disturbing, even possessing, the minds of pilots and sea captains passing through the area. Exorcists have endeavoured to free these troubled souls. One of them is Dr Kenneth McCall, a surgeon

and psychiatrist who discovered an unusual power of prayer while working as a missionary in China. He travelled to the United States to demonstrate his gift. It was while returning from giving a lecture tour there in 1946 that he found himself stranded on a banana boat in the Sargasso Sea (located in the eastern part of the Triangle). The ship's engine had failed and they drifted for about five days. Fortunately the weather was calm. There was a peaceful atmosphere. Dr McCall started to hear singing and assumed the crew were keeping themselves happy while they waited for help. The psychiatrist recognised the tune as a negro spiritual. But when he went to check, none of the crew were, or had been, singing at all, nor was there a radio or record player on board. Yet he and his wife Frances both heard a faint chanting for several days until help arrived and they were back on their way. It seemed clear to the doctor that these chants must have come from the souls of past slaves abandoned at sea.

Roman Centurion Pining for Princess
Ghost of the causeway to West Mersea Island

For hundreds of years the Romans occupied Britain. They built towns, amenities and their famous straight roads linking them all together. The Romans lived and died here, and thousands were buried. The capital of Roman Britain was Colchester near the Essex marshes. One of the roads out of the city ran east to West Mersea Island. In fact the modern road follows the old route taken by a causeway the Romans built.

The island used to be a retirement place for soldiers when they finished service in the Roman army. According to tradition a princess lived on the island and was married to a Roman centurion. At one end of the causeway there is an ancient tumulus, or burial mound, Saxon in origin but containing Roman remains, and here she is thought to have been entombed.

The causeway is said to be haunted by the Roman centurion. Several locals claim interesting sightings and sounds. Jill Smeaton who lives nearby gave one account. On the night of the autumn equinox, September 23, in 1987, she heard a noise in the early hours of the morning that woke her with a start. She sat up in bed and could hear the sound of two unshod horses passing outside her bungalow window followed by the rumble of a heavy wagon, so heavy in fact they caused the walls to shake. Her husband slept through it but her friend, who was in the next room, heard the same noise. Thinking her own horses must have escaped, Jill and her friend rushed outside but saw nothing unusual. She checked her horses and they were grazing as

Roman centurian

though nothing had happened.

Others have reported similar auditory experiences.

Some claim to have actually seen the centurion. One local resident, Alfred, described an experience when he was returning from Colchester one night. It was misty, he said, and all of a sudden at the side of the road, from between a pond and a haystack, emerged a figure. It appeared to be walking towards the burial mound and looked like a Roman centurion. It wore a helmet with an eagle on the front, a uniform, shield and sword, though his legs were not visible. Alfred and his friends stopped the car, jumped out but the figure had quickly reached the mound where there was an opening. The centurion turned to them and then vanished.

STONE TAPE THEORY

What possible explanations are there for these bizarre events, which witnesses swear are real experiences? Some academics claim there is one credible theory to explain the recurrence of sights and sounds that relate to so long ago. Archie Roy, Professor of Astronomy, says, 'We have to postulate that some very emotional scene has somehow become registered on the environment, almost like a sort of psychic video has been created. Someone who comes along who is sensitive enough acts as a sort of psychic video player and will actually play that "tape" and see the figures or perhaps even hear the voices. It is nothing to do with the people who were originally there, they're no longer there. It's simply a record.'

Jim Lyons, a research physicist, says that if you imagine some traumatic experience such as a decapitation, the 'energy liberated at that point in time is in effect transmitted, expelled into the surrounding material... and stored in that material. These subtle energies, a series of vibrational energies, can in fact then be read out at some later time. This concept is known as Stone Tape Theory.

The opinion of these two experts is that the ghost-like sights and sounds are not in fact ghosts as we traditionally conceive them but constitute a kind of entrapment of actual historical phenomena which can still be experienced today. Could this be a new understanding of what ghosts are?

Hairy Hands of Dartmoor

Inexplicable accidents on the Postbridge Road

From 1910 onwards a series of unusual accidents occurred on the road across Dartmoor between Postbridge and Two Bridges, now the B3212. In each case the victims reported the sensation of having their steering wheel or handle bars pulled to one side causing their car or bike to swerve violently and crash. The police could offer no explanation. Matters came to a head in 1921 when Dr Helby, medical officer to Dartmoor prison, was killed on the same stretch of road. He was travelling on a motorbike when he lost control in a similar manner. His two young daughters, who were riding in the sidecar, survived to tell of the incident.

Then the following year a sensational twist was added to the next incident there. This time an army captain reported feeling a pair of invisible hands grab him as he rode his motorbike, causing him to veer on to the moor. When he picked himself up there was no sign of anyone about.

Dartmoor, near Postbridge

He was completely alone on an open road.

Things then became stranger still. When Florence Warwick, aged 28, was driving here one evening after a sightseeing tour her car suddenly started to vibrate, so she pulled over and consulted the manual. While looking down at the handbook, she recalled, 'A cold feeling suddenly came over me. I felt as if I was being watched. I looked up and saw a pair of huge, hairy hands pressed against the windscreen. I tried to scream, but couldn't. I was frozen with fear.' In terror Florence could do nothing but watch these disembodied hands creep across the windscreen. With no one around to call on for help she was trapped, 'It was horrible,' she said. 'They were just inches away. After what seemed a lifetime, I heard myself cry out and the hands seemed to vanish.'

Fortunately she could start the car. The juddering seemed to have stopped so she went on her way without further ado to where she was staying with friends in Torbay, half an hour away. Still shaken on arrival, she described what happened. Florence

then learnt that the Postbridge road was believed to be cursed and had been haunted for many years.

Road improvements

Once news of these incidents reached the national press, an investigation was conducted about the danger of the road to motorists. Duly the local authority was required to make improvements and the camber was levelled out. It was hoped this correction to the road would put an end to the string of accidents.

Yet soon afterwards another incident happened, this time involving a caravan. A fog had descended rapidly, as can happen on Dartmoor, making it impossible to drive. The couple with the caravan pulled over into a lay-by. After cooking a meal, they decided to put their heads down. Not long after falling asleep the woman was woken by the noise of scratching outside the caravan. Thinking it must be a pony or stray dog from the moor, she got up to take a look. Then, as with Florence Warwick in the previous account, she felt a chill around her as her eye was taken to a window above the bunk where her husband slept. There, to her horror, she saw a large pair of hairy hands creeping across the glass. Being a Catholic, she made a sign of the cross and the hands disappeared.

More road accidents occurred at the spot, again with no reasonable cause attributable. Even walkers have reported feeling a strange sensation of unease, temporarily, which would fade after a few minutes. No explanations were ever found for the 'hairy hands'. Psychic investigators attribute the phenomenon to an accident in which there died an unnamed man whose spirit is awakened in particular, though unknown, conditions.

The Phantom Hitchhiker

Figures looming in the headlights

A girl stands in the rain on a dark night by the side of the road, and is glimpsed in the headlights of a passing car. The driver, a man, stops and offers her a lift. She, attractive, mumbles a word of thanks but is clearly in a depressed state and stays silent on the journey.

From then on, the details vary from one account to another, but the story of the phantom hitchhiker is a worldwide phenomenon, though especially prevalent in the US. One version of the legend continues as follows.

The driver, a young man looking for love, offers the shivering girl his white jumper which he has on the back seat. She gratefully receives with a smile. The hitchhiker says she must get back to see her parents, and the driver then notices her face and hands are badly scratched. He asks what has happened and she explains that her car came off the road and ended up in a ditch. She had been standing on the side of the road for ages hoping for help.

He says he is perfectly willing to take her directly to her parents' house which, anyway, is only a few miles up the road. After a short while, she points to the lights on inside a house at the end of a short lane, and asks him to stop, saying she can walk from here. Before he has a chance even to ask her name, she is out of the car and gone.

As the young man drives on, he

remembers that the girl still has his sweater. This will be the excuse for him to return in the hope of meeting her again. Two days later he does just that, and knocks on the door of the house the girl indicated. An elderly lady opens the door and invites him in. As his eyes rove around the interior they fasten on a portrait photograph of the girl hitchhiker. When the old lady sees him looking at it she begins to weep, saying that her dear daughter is still trying to come home after being killed in a car accident on a dark rainy night 40 years ago. She was just 19 at the time.

The man makes his excuse and leaves, thinking the old lady must be mad. Clearly the girl he picked up just two days ago was alive. However, as he passes a cemetery something white billowing on the top of a gravestone catches his attention. He stops to investigate. When he walks up to the grave he is aghast to discover that the white thing is in fact his sweater he had lent the hitchhiker. Furthermore it is draped over a headstone that reads of a 19 year-old girl who died tragically 40 years ago.

GHOST IN THE MACHINE

Mystery of the *Mary Celeste*
Strange desertion in the Azores

When crew aboard the *Dei Gratia* spotted the *Mary Celeste* drifting some 600 miles west of Portugal, they could not believe what they were about to find. It was December 3, 1872, and they were on their way to Gibraltar. Apprehensive and ready with arms, a detachment set off in a rowing boat to investigate. Fearing an encounter with pirates or a scene of devastation, the sailors were amazed instead to discover a scene of calm normality as if the ship were in running order. The only strange thing was that no one was aboard.

Neither Captain Benjamin Briggs, his wife and young daughter, nor any of the crew of seven were present. In fact most things, including the ship's cargo of alcohol, appeared to be intact. Washing hung on the line in the crew's quarters; in the captain's cabin a sewing machine

Mary Celeste

was apparently in use on a table, and sheet music stood on a rosewood melodeon. It was as though an emergency had arisen and the ship been abandoned. Yet there was little to point to a hasty departure. The last entry in the log was made ten days earlier, when the captain recorded sight of the Azores and noted his bearings.

Fact or fiction?

Much of the legendary fame attached to the discovery of the *Mary Celeste* may be attributed to the author Sir Arthur Conan Doyle who wrote an embellished story about the event, *J Habakuk Jephson's Statement*. Many of the details of the real account were altered with artistic licence but became confused with reality in public minds. A breakfast was not found half-eaten, for instance, as the

Sir Arthur Conan Doyle

popular version has it, with Captain Briggs's boiled egg already topped for consumption. The place was not completely ship-shape either: the galley was found in a mess and the stove wrenched forward. Hatches were open and a fair depth of water had penetrated the bilge, though this was to be expected of a timber-framed ship.

To Gibraltar

Captain Morehouse of the *Dei Gratia* decided to tow the ship to his destination in the hope of being able to claim salvage money for the cargo. En route he could not help but turn over in his mind the possibilities of what might have happened.

Could it have been abandoned in a storm? The ship sustained no structural damage, and besides, surely more articles would have been thrown about the place. Was there perhaps a mutiny? Although there was no obvious sign of a struggle, no lifeboats were found, if the ship had them in the first place. The only cargo worth the trouble of mutinying over – ten casks of alcohol – remained on board.

Most puzzling of all was how the *Mary Celeste* had remained on course for ten days without being manned. Indeed, the sails were set on a starboard tack and it would have been impossible for the ship to sail on that course to where it was found. On the evidence it seemed that somehow the *Mary Celeste* had been steered after its personnel had disappeared.

On arrival in Gibraltar, an enquiry was held. The ship had set sail from New York on November 7, 1872, bound for Genoa in Italy. The outcome was inconclusive, but what did emerge was the barrels, originally thought to be full, were in fact found to be empty. Did the entire crew go on a heavy drinking binge until all was consumed and then take off in the lifeboats, never to be seen again? The mystery was never solved. The ship was sold but crews refused to sail in her believing it to be cursed. Eventually, after being sold many times over, the *Mary Celeste* ran aground off the coast of Haiti in the Caribbean.

Some have speculated that the entire crew fell subject to a strange ghostly force that overwhelmed the vessel and continued sailing it without human aid. Some even believe the crew became victims of an alien abduction.

GHOST SHIPS

Spectral ships and boats are well known lore in sea-faring societies. Some tribal cultures believe such vessels provide the means of transport for souls of the dead to the realm of the afterlife. Legends of phantom ships appear in European and American folklore, especially associated with some disaster at sea. Ghostly vessels are believed to haunt the scene of the disaster, sometimes re-enacting the final moments. Ghost ships continue to be reported, especially off the Atlantic coast.

Deadly Queen Mary
Haunted ocean liner

The luxury ocean liner *Queen Mary* now lies serene in dry dock at Long Beach, California. Yet

HMS Queen Mary

many people claim to have heard and seen phantoms associated with its history. The ship was in service for more than 30 years from 1936, during which 41 passengers and at least 16 members of crew died at sea, either from illness or by tragic accident.

Its size and speed in the water made the ship a useful asset during the Second World War, transporting up to 16,000 American troops to and from Europe. Painted in inconspicuous battle grey, the liner was nicknamed the 'Grey Ghost' for its ability to elude German U-boats. However this power and swiftness was also the undoing of an ally when the ship accidentally struck its escort HMS *Curacao*, slicing the vessel in two and drowning all 300 of its crew.

Since the *Queen Mary* was permanently docked in 1967, visitors have reported sounds of terrible

HMS Curacao

screams coming from the bows and of heavy metal wrenching apart, perhaps echoes of that awful night when the *Curacao* was hit.

Sightings of officers and crew members in the passageways have also been reported. The most common apparition is of the unfortunate 18 year-old John Pedder who was crushed to death by hydraulic door number 13 in the engine room during a drill. Visions of a young man in blue overalls are sometimes seen on the catwalks of the engine room before vanishing.

Various rooms in the passengers' luxury apartments are believed to be haunted, including the First Class Suite where a man in a 1930s suit has been spotted, and in the Queen's salon where the ghost of a young woman in a white dress has been seen lounging. One cabin in particular, however, seems to be more haunted than any other: Room B340. So much disturbing activity has been reported of this cabin, concerning an eight-year-old girl who died there, that it is no longer let out.

Flight 401 to Miami
Crash in the Everglades

On the night of December 29, 1972, Eastern Air Lines Flight 401 was approaching Miami and preparing to land. Captain Bob Loft and flight engineer Don Repo were going about their usual routine when a warning light flashed up indicating a problem with the landing equipment. As the captain's attention was distracted away from his primary task of piloting the plane, he did not realise quite how fast they were descending and within minutes crashed into the swamp of the Florida Everglades. Of the 176 people on board, 101 were killed on impact. The captain survived the crash itself but died before he could be pulled from the wreckage. Don Repo died a day later.

As the airplane landed on water some parts remained undamaged and were salvaged by the US airline to be used in its other aircraft. Soon after these parts had been redistributed, crew from the planes in which those parts had been fitted began reporting strange sightings of Bob Loft and Don Repo on board.

The ghost of Captain Loft was once seen sitting in the First Class section talking to the vice-president of Eastern Air Lines. On another occasion a stewardess saw him without knowing it to be Captain Loft. When she reported the unidentified person, the pilot immediately recognised the description as Loft. At that point the ghost vanished before the eyes of several witnesses.

In many cases the ghostly presence appears to be aimed at helping the crew, warning them about safety, the risk of fire hazard and so on. It was as though the technical fault that caused Flight 401 to crash weighed so heavily on the spirits of the two deceased airmen that they had returned to help future crews avoid similar ghastly accidents. Messages of warning would sound over the public address system, the plane's power would suddenly surge in difficult conditions, and once apparently a tool mysteriously appeared in the hand of an operative doing some maintenance work.

The frequency of phantom appearances reached such a level

that Eastern Air Lines offered its staff counselling at its own expense in an effort to overcome the matter. When that made little or no difference the airline company decided the only course of action was to remove the parts recycled from the Tristar L-1011 jet of Flight 401.

Almost immediately all sightings and ghostly effects ceased. The phenomenon remains a mystery and became the subject of a bestseller, *The Ghost of Flight 401,* in which John Fuller relates this remarkable story.

Spectres at London Airport
Panting, VIP lounge and Runway One

Many staff at Heathrow have been alarmed by a sound like a dog panting. It usually occurs outside, often at a point said to be haunted by Dick Turpin. One employee of Pan America described a time when she had just left her car in the staff park when a heavy breathing, like a panting animal sounded behind her. She turned but nothing was there, yet the sensation continued. Interestingly, a man and woman nearby had moved away from her because they too had felt the same experience. The employee spoke about this to an

London Heathrow Airport

airline engineer who said she wasn't the first to experience such noises. Yet there was no reasonable explanation for them.

Another spectral presence has been reported at Heathrow, this one visible. It does not pant, or indeed make any sound, but is just as unsettling. It – or rather he – has appeared in the VIP suite at the airport's European Terminal. This lounge is reserved for dignitaries of state. Once a visiting diplomat from an African high commission was said to have been terrified by the sight of a phantom pair of trousers. They were light grey, as though the bottom half of a suit. A supervisor who operates regularly in the area says she caught sight of a ghost in a light grey suit. It wasn't there for long. 'When I looked again, it had vanished,' she said. 'There was no way he could have got out of the lounge without coming past me. I'm not afraid. I think he's friendly.'

Runway One

On March 2, 1948, a DC3 plane crashed on Runway One and burst into flames, killing 22 passengers. Many years later, one evening in 1970, Police Inspector Leslie Alton received an alert that the airport radar was showing someone walking on the same runway. The inspector headed a search party of three squad cars and a fire engine. Guided by radio link to the radar, the police endeavoured to close in on the miscreant. However, on the ground there was no visible sign of anyone, yet the radar was tracking someone. Having searched up and down the runway and, according to the radar operatives, run over the trespasser, the police gave up their ordeal.

Several night-shift workers had apparently also seen a figure outside, about six feet tall, wearing a bowler hat and cavalry twill trousers, who seemed to be looking for something. A spiritualist independently described the figure as a Guardsman. On checking the files recording the 1948 crash, it was noted that as rescue workers searched the wreckage, a man in a bowler hat had come up to them and asked if they had seen his briefcase. Could this 'person' have actually been a phantom that reappeared on the runway that night in 1970?

Haunting the Skies
The Phantom Lancaster bomber

In 2004 numerous sightings of a low-flying plane over the town of Barnoldswick in Yorkshire led to speculation that it must have been a spectral Avro Lancaster bomber of the kind used successfully in the Second World War. The bomber is best known for the part it played in a raid of the Ruhr Valley dams in Germany, an event dramatised in the film, *The Dambusters.*

One morning in January 2004 a visitor to Barnoldswick was aghast to see a large grey military aircraft loom out of the mist, silently, near the Rolls Royce factory. The plane was flying so low over the houses that the onlooker, Moira Thwaites,

a retired policewoman, was afraid it might hit the car she and her partner were travelling in. Expecting to hear a thunderous crash at any moment, they looked back after pulling over to see or hear nothing at all.

Convinced they had just seen a wartime bomber, the couple made local enquiries. It was suggested that the aircraft might have been involved in an RAF training exercise using propeller-powered aircraft such as the Hercules transporters. But there is a strict regulation on altitude for flying, especially over a town of 10,000 or so residents.

When the local newspaper, *The Craven Herald,* ran the story several other witnesses came forward saying they too had seen the mysterious plane. The description emerging

Barnoldswick Lancashire

- 104 -

also differed in key details from a Hercules: the sighted aircraft having a dual tail fin, like the Lancaster bomber, not one as with the Hercules, and the general impression was of a much more dated design.

Is it possible that a commemorative flight was organized by Rolls Royce, once partners in the manufacture of the Avro Lancaster at their factory at nearby Bankfield? A Rolls Royce source confirmed they own a spitfire which they fly from time to time, but this is a much smaller plane altogether, an agile fighter plane not a heavy bomber. Besides, there is known to be only one Lancaster left in Europe still capable of flying and that is based at Coningsby in Lincolnshire.

Mrs Thwaites and her partner, among others, were at a loss for an explanation. They contacted a local historical research group at Skipton whose president, Donald Cooper, declared there had been several incidents reported in Yorkshire of phantom aircraft. He offered no explanation as such, but did say

There is a lot of electrical energy and physics that we are not even aware of surrounding the earth and a site like Rolls Royce generates a great deal of energy. Mrs Thwaites is adamant what she saw was a plane, but whether it was something breaking through another dimension or paranormal activity I cannot tell her.

Donald Cooper, quoted in *The Craven Herald*.

Mr Cooper then added that the previous week a national newspaper had run an article about 'time slips', reporting a number of cases in which people claimed to have seen Second-World-War aircraft apparently operating missions, usually silently, as though time had slipped back 60 years.

Nothing more was reported for another two years, until February 2006, when further sightings of the bomber emerged. *The Craven Herald* again ran a story about a resident of Skipton who had spotted a plane looking like a Lancaster bomber that fitted the previous description. It was grey with no markings, silent, and headed towards a short airstrip at Barnoldswick. Now what also emerged was that this airfield was once the scene of an emergency landing during the war. One elderly gentleman remembered the occasion, when he was a boy, saying the army and police moved in quickly to seal off the area and no one could get a look. Was this plane a Lancaster? Did it perhaps crash land and leave behind some sort of phantom for posterity? We don't know. Certainly a lot of people have claimed, in earnest, to witness these strange sightings.

Phantom Full Beamer
Re-enacted car accident in Surrey

A busy stretch of the A3 dual carriageway out of London was the scene of a reported accident on December 11, 2002. Several witnesses phoned the police to say they had seen a car with headlights on full beam veer off the road near Burpham in Surrey. When the police investigated, there was no immediate sign of a crash on or beside the road.

Only on further searching did they in fact discover the wreckage of a car buried in the undergrowth, close to the reported sighting.

Clearly this was an old accident

that had gone undiscovered. The car, a Vauxhall Astra, was nose down entangled in branches and weeds. A body was found inside in a near skeletal condition. Dental tests later revealed the identity of the man as Christopher Chandler of West London who was wanted by police in connection with an armed robbery in July of that year, after which he was reported missing by his brother.

Surrey police believe the accident happened in July and the car had lain undetected since then because it was so well hidden in an overgrown ditch by the roadside. No other vehicle was involved. It was noted that the battery was flat and the headlamps were switched to the full beam position.

The several motorists who reported the incident they had seen on December 11 were left wondering if they had seen some sort of ghostly replay of the crash in July.

St Louis Ghost Train
Lights in the dark

An enduring mystery in Saskatchewan in Canada is the ghost train of St Louis. For many years a strange light moves fast up and down an old abandoned railway line at night (though one witness claims to have seen it in daylight too). The 'train' varies in colour and intensity along the route taken just north of St Louis where the tracks no longer lie, having been removed a long time ago.

When some friends came to visit Serge and Gail Gareau, who grew up in the vicinity of St Louis, the hosts offered them some unusual entertainment: to hunt a ghost train. Now living in the village of Saskatoon, Gareau drove them all the 80 miles to St Louis one autumn evening. If the train is going to be seen at all, it was usually known to come by at around midnight. They arrived in good time and waited beside the abandoned railway. After a long time of nothing happening, suddenly a light appeared on the horizon. It looked just like a train was approaching. Beneath the main white beam a smaller red light shone as well. With great excitement the two couples watched the light apparently approaching yet never reaching them. They decided to drive towards the light along a dirt track beside the old

railway line, keeping a steady watch on it through their windscreen. After what seemed like a long time driving, the light suddenly disappeared. They looked behind them and there it was! One member of the party became scared and they decided to head back home, though enthralled by this encounter.

Local knowledge of the strange phenomenon had spawned various legends about it. One was that a train conductor had been struck by a train and decapitated while carrying out a routine check of the track. The smaller red light seen with the ghost train is thought to be the lantern the conductor carried.

At some later point the mayor of St Louis, Emile Lussier, who now runs a hotel by the old track, thought it was time to put this matter to the test. As far as he was aware no one had actually walked the old railway track, fearing it to be too dangerous of course. Now Lussier dared his brother-in-law to do just this, to walk this route, and carry on walking even into the light! They agreed and shook hands.

The intrepid pair set out and

walked about a mile without seeing anything. Then suddenly the light appeared right at their heels, with terrifying intensity, like an enraged creature. It cast strong shadows and then as quickly as it appeared it vanished again. Relieved somewhat to still be alive, the two men turned round and headed back.

With the town abuzz with excitement on hearing their news, it was not long before others wanted to see for themselves. Lussier's son and friends went there with his father. Wishing to witness the experience on their own, Emile drove them to the beginning of the old track and he remained there while the boys set off up the track. On this occasion, something different happened. The boys were well out of site when suddenly a huge orb of light lit up the immediate surroundings, yet the boys did not see that.

The variety of the lights witnessed has prompted investigators to conclude that the source cannot be a phantom train but some sort of strange phenomena which they cannot explain. Others maintain there is a spectral link with the conductor who was killed in the train accident.

EARTH LIGHTS

Unexplained lights, known as Earth Lights, that appear above ground level have caused a good deal of puzzlement over the years. Although they are a hot topic of discussion among current paranormal investigators, the lights have been appearing for centuries. In medieval times they were believed to be 'fairy lights', often with mischievous intent which could lead travellers astray. The lights vary in size, shape and intensity, and can be any colour. They can appear as luminous vapours with glowing tails. Some are associated with vibrational sounds, others even explode. There are various scientific attempts at explanation: one suggests the lights occur near geological fault lines during earthquake activity; another says electrical charges are emitted in the atmosphere or from the ground itself, and light up in the dark. So far no compelling answer has been put forward. Many paranormal investigators are convinced the lights are linked to spirits.

PHANTOMS OF THE STAGE

Dressing Room Haunt
Celebrity returns to the Adelphi

The Adelphi Theatre in the West End of London was a popular venue for Victorian audiences and a much loved actor there was William Terriss. He led a colourful life off stage as well as on it. His trademark garb was a sleek pair of light grey gloves with which he would perform most roles. His popularity, however, also engendered a certain envy among his peers. One night in December 1897, as he led another successful run, this time of a thriller called *Secret Service,* he went downstairs to unlock the stage door in Maiden Lane, when an actor he knew came forward and stabbed Terriss fatally. The murderer, Richard Prince, had been sacked from the Adelphi for alcoholism and ever since had born a grudge against the profession and in particular the adulation of its most charismatic performer. Prince was convicted of murder and spent the rest of his days in Broadmoor Prison penning plays which were never staged.

As Terriss lay dying in the arms of his leading lady Jessie Milward, he vowed to 'come back'. It was in 1928 when his dying words first came

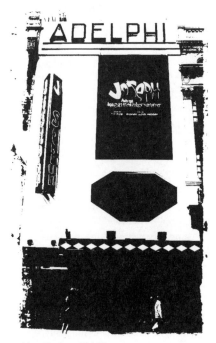

Adam Brothers Adelphi

William Terriss

true. A visitor to London who did not know of the actor saw a figure dressed in grey Victorian clothes suddenly disappear in Maiden Lane. He later identified the figure from photographs as William Terriss.

In the same year an actress preparing to go on stage felt the sofa in her dressing room move, as though being shaken by an invisible force. Then her arm was seized, so hard that it left a bruise. The lights flickered on and off, and she saw a green light above her mirror. When the actress described these alarming events to her dresser, she explained that the room used to belong to Jessie Milward. Was it now the turn of William Terriss to be envious, that no longer was his favourite actress the leading lady?

Dandy in the Dress Circle
Lurking shadows in Drury Lane

London's oldest playhouse, Theatre Royal Drury Lane, built in 1663, was filled with audiences who liked nothing more than a good old dose of murder and intrigue. Jacobean drama gave them just that. Charles II granted the playhouse its royal charter and is said to have been 'seen' on occasions. But the most frequent visiting ghost is an unknown gentleman of the 18th century. Dressed in dapper grey and tricorn hat, powdered wig and sword, the fellow has been seen stalking the dress circle during rehearsals. Strolling from one end of the balcony to

Drury Lane interior

another the dandy would then vanish onto the wall. However, this ghost has no malevolence; indeed his appearance is usually taken to be good luck for the show. Many cleaners swear to have seen the figure lurking about outside the hours of performance. Some have speculated that he is linked to an eerie discovery in 1860 when labourers making alterations found a skeleton inside a hollow brick wall with a dagger still stuck between the ribs.

The Ghoul and the Bard
Shakespeare and ghosts

The supernatural was a source of intrigue to William Shakespeare. Several of his plays – *Macbeth, The Tempest, A Midsummer Night's Dream* and *Hamlet* – all feature ghostly characters. Ghosts and the afterlife were a part of the fabric of Elizabethan life. Belief in purgatory

A Midsummer Night's Dream by Henry Fuseli

The Tempest *by George Romney*

meant spirits might frequently return to the world on special missions, and that they should be assisted in their purpose (an idea that developed into Spiritualism in the Victorian era). In his tragedy Shakespeare wrote that Hamlet was doomed to walk the night 'till the foul crimes done in my days are burnt and purg'd away' (Act 1, Scene 5, verses 12-13). Interestingly only he could see the ghost of his father, Claudia could not.

Shakespeare was familiar with the classic ghost stories of his age and made a point of visiting haunted sites in the hope of experiencing the supernatural. In the true sense of the word, he was a religious writer, 'who is aware, and makes his spectators aware, of the mystery of things' (*Shakespeare For All Time,* Stanley Wells, London, 2002). Even in the plays where there is no direct spectral reference, he nevertheless cleverly

William Shakespeare

he imagined – of an emaciated old woman arriving on the doorstep trembling in the throes of death – might have unsettled local residents. After Poe's departure, the dwelling became a subject of rumours of sightings of strange things within. Shadows of a figure working at a desk were seen on the second floor, not the attic, when the building was supposed to be vacant. A reported burglary brought the police to investigate and they observed a phantom light slowly ascending from a ground floor window to windows at higher floors, yet on inspection no light was found, nor anyone who

suggests the interplay of supernatural forces in human lives – and clearly he was addressing an audience all too ready to believe in ghostly realities.

Spooks in Amity Street
Edgar Allan Poe's house

Edgar Allan Poe

A little house in Baltimore was once occupied by the mystery author Edgar Allan Poe. During his stay at 203 North Amity Street from 1832 to 1835, no unusual phenomena was reported. The writer habitually sat in the attic to write his ghost stories, most famously *The Fall of the House of Usher*. The gruesome tales

Virginia Poe Clemm

could have been using a torch.

Even by day the house was spooky. A portrait of Poe's wife, painted while lying dead in her coffin, hung on the wall, her eyes following the visitor round the room. Poe himself had a morbid obsession with premature burial, a theme that crops up in many of his horror stories, and eventually ended his life in a mental asylum.

When his house became a museum, the curator reported various unusual phenomena from particular rooms, especially those once occupied by Poe's grandmother and then his cousin, Virginia Clemm, later his wife.

Doors and windows would open by themselves. Visitors to the museum have been tapped on the shoulder and voices heard. There has also been a sighting of an old lady with long grey hair dressed in contemporary clothing drifting through the grandmother's former room. The house has acquired such a haunted reputation that even gangs of robbers now steer clear of it.

Sir Arthur Conan Doyle and Spiritualism
Master of detective stories pursues ultimate mystery

A movement known as Spiritualism fired Victorian imaginations when self-proclaimed psychics claimed to make contact with spirits of the dead. The craze began in 1848 with the Fox Sisters who conducted séances in which responses to their questions were said to be received by audible knockings, one for 'yes', two for 'no'. Despite later being exposed as frauds – their technique involved an unusual ability to click their toes – other mediums made similar claims, some more convincing than others, and some genuine.

One of the most famous exponents was the author of the Sherlock Holmes murder mysteries, Sir Arthur Conan Doyle, whose whole-hearted conversion to Spiritualism in the early years of the First World War won many followers. However, his pursuit of the paranormal suffered a setback when the escapologist Harry Houdini, at first an ally, remained sceptical of the psychic power Doyle ascribed to him.

It was said that the deaths of several relatives of Doyle on the Front Line, and ultimately that of his son, Kingsley, two weeks before Armistice, affected his mental stability. The novelist claimed in one séance to have heard his dead son speak to him. He was also convinced that spirit messages could be delivered from beyond the grave by a process known as Automatic Writing. A

Arthur Conan Doyle

practitioner of this skill, Lily Loder-Symonds, is said to have written in the unmistakeable style of Doyle's brother-in-law, Malcolm Leckie, who had been killed a month earlier in the war, in April 1915. During the communication, Doyle was staggered to receive correct answers to his personal questions, answers which Lily could not possibly have known.

After the 1920s the movement lost momentum, though revived periodically. However, its core concern with making contact with the dead is still very much a live issue today.

GHOST BOOKS AND FILMS

The Flying Dutchman
Legends of a phantom ship

The legend of the *Flying Dutchman* is the classic phantom-ship ghost story. Observed from afar emerging out of a mist, the tall-masted ghost ship glows with unearthly power and is usually regarded as an omen of disaster.

Richard Wagner

The original story is Dutch. A captain, named van Straaten, claimed to be able to sail round the treacherous Cape of Good Hope even in a storm. Alas, neither captain nor any member of crew survived the ordeal but the ship sailed on, forever traversing the oceans.

The story was popularized as an opera by Richard Wagner, *Der Fliegender Hallander*, in 1843. In this version the captain, Hendrik Vanderdecken, curses God who condemns him to sail the seas until doomsday.

A tradition of sightings of the *Flying Dutchman* around the seas of the Cape of Good Hope has developed since 1923 when an apparition of the phantom ship was proclaimed. The account is recorded by a member of the Society of Psychical Research, Sir Ernest Bennett. Bennett attempted to explain the phenomenon in a theory that some sort of consciousness survives death and is able to project images perceptible to the human eye. Although there was interest in the idea at the time, little support for it remains.

According to Sir Walter Scott, sight of the *Flying Dutchman* is a portent of death and disaster for those sailors who witness it. It was said that as a young sailor the future George V had an apparition of the *Flying Dutchman* in 1880 while sailing off the coast of Australia aboard the flagship

Wagner Fliegende Hollander

Inconstant. However, this turns out to be untrue. Rather, the vision was allegedly seen by other members of the crew. They described a strangely red, glowing phantom ship some 200 yards away. Sceptics suggest that the apparition was merely an optical illusion, a mirage involving perhaps phosphorescence. What is undeniable is that one of the sailors who claimed to see the *Flying Dutchman* died shortly afterwards in an accident.

The Amityville Haunting
Horror or hoax?

Much controversy was generated by the publication of Jay Anson's book, *The Amityville Horror*, in 1977. If it had simply been another 'horror' novel, no one would have thought much about it. But it was the subtitle, *A True Story*, that caused the stir. In December 1975 a couple, George and Kathleen Lutz, bought a house, 112 Ocean Avenue, in a suburban neighbourhood on Long Island, New York. It was a large elegant place, of Dutch Colonial style, and had been empty for the past 13 months. The reason: it was last occupied by Ronald DeFeo, who had shot dead six members of his family at this address.

When the agent told the couple about this matter as they viewed the property, they decided it would not be a problem and reckoned they could live with it. As a precaution they apparently called in a priest to bless the house. In a later interview during an inquest into the events that happened here, the priest vowed that while conducting his blessing had heard a voice say, 'Get out'. Not only this but he felt a slap on his face and blistering of the hands. He did, however, stop short of attributing these phenomena to the paranormal.

A series of unsettling things happened, apparently, to the couple and their family, made up of respective step-children.

Much of the haunting reported was experienced by George. He would wake in the middle of the night and hear noises: the front door would slam, yet on inspection there was nothing, their dog fast asleep as usual. Sometimes he would hear German marching tunes, but no one

Amityville House

else would. He also strangely felt the compunction at 3am to go and check the boathouse at the end of the garden and would find nothing there. But when he turned to return he once saw a pair of red demonic eyes at the window of his five-year old daughter's bedroom. Rushing up to her, again there would be nothing untoward – his daughter, Missy, soundly asleep. Independently Missy developed an imaginary friend, which she described as being a pig-like creature with glowing red eyes.

Many other 'symptoms' of the paranormal with a horror edge to them were narrated in the book. After 28 days of these experiences, the Lutz family had had enough and moved out. A rash of publicity blew up about the whole story, reporters became avid for snippets of their lifestyle and inevitably the Lutzes felt misrepresented in articles. They filed a lawsuit in 1977 and a countersuit followed that. In these two cases many elements of the Lutz story were challenged and in some instances the evidence was profoundly questionable. In one affidavit the priest, Father Pecoraro, claimed the only contact he ever had with the Lutzes was over the telephone, yet in interviews he stood by his original statements. The Lutzes had claimed that doors, locks and windows had been damaged by paranormal forces, yet the next occupants of the house said they were in perfectly good condition, and looked original. The Lutzes had even asserted that cloven hoofed footprints, as though belonging to a demonic pig, had appeared in the snow on 1 January, yet weather reports at that time gave no indication of snow having fallen.

Under stern interrogation, George Lutz finally conceded that the facts in the book were only 'mostly true'. The lawyer, William Webber, acting in defence of Ronald DeFoe also declared, 'I know this book is a hoax. We created this horror story over many bottles of wine.' This statement refers to a meeting he had with George and Kathleen Lutz in which they discussed the ideas that would become the stuff of Anson's book. But to the end, George Lutz insisted, 'It's

certainly not a hoax. It's real easy to call something a hoax. I wish it was. It's not.' Hoax or not, the goings-on at 112 Ocean Avenue certainly provided rich material for Hollywood success at the box-office when the movie appeared in 1979.

The Hound of the Baskervilles
Snarling dogs of terror

The inspiration for Sir Arthur Conan Doyle's horror novel, *The Hound of the Baskervilles,* derived from a tour in 1901 of Dartmoor and its villages that huddle against the howling wind. The remote hinterland, the treacherous bogs, and often damp, foggy air provide the perfect breeding ground for ghostly legends of marauding packs of hounds. It must have been thrilling for the author to allow his imagination free rein over the mirey landscape suggestive of evil creatures. Doyle's tour guide was his coachman, a local man named Harry Baskerville. So impressed was the novelist by the aristocratic sound of his name that he asked the driver if could use his name in a new story. Thus was born the famous spine-chiller.

One legend that the novelist probably encountered on his travels concerned the devilish squire Richard Cabell of Buckfastleigh. It is said that his death in 1677 was accompanied by a vision of phantom hounds bounding from deepest Dartmoor to drag Cabell's soul to hell. Such was the man's reputation, the locals were anxious not to be haunted by his return in ghostly form. The coffin was first buried in Buckfastleigh churchyard under a heavy stone. Over this was placed an altar tomb. Then immovable iron bars were installed around the tomb and the whole ensemble enclosed within a stone hut for good measure.

Alas the fortifications did not work. On stormy nights a pack of fiendish hounds were said to be heard baying at his tomb until the squire would emerge from the grave and drive them across the moor curdling the blood of any unfortunate wayfarer they may encounter.

BLACK SHUCK

British folklore is full of legends about spectral black dogs – known as Black Shuck in some counties, especially in East Anglia. His appearance is often regarded as a bad omen, usually of death. The

Black Dog – shuck

origins of the name are mysterious. The idea may have stemmed from the Celtic legends of Arawn, whose hounds preyed on the souls of the dead. Black Shuck is reported to be a large dog with red or yellow eyes and sometimes a collar made of chain that rattles with intent. It is said to roam graveyards and quiet country roads, and howl dreadfully on stormy nights.

POETS AND THE IMAGINATION

Lord Byron
Goblin friar of Newstead Abbey

Newstead Abbey from Morris's Seats

Lord Byron was fascinated by ghosts and the supernatural. He lived in an age when Gothic horror novels were fashionable. He investigated many accounts of hauntings himself. In his own experience, he is said to have witnessed a phantom monk in their family home at Newstead Abbey. Lying within Sherwood Forest of Nottinghamshire, Newstead was

Byron 1824

originally a monastery of Augustinian black-robed monks of the 12th century. Byron recalls meeting a 'goblin friar', which he took to be an ill omen for the family, in his poem *Don Juan*:

> It was no mouse, but lo! a monk array'd
> in cowl and beads and dusky garb,
> appear'd,
> Now in the moonlight, and now lapsed
> in shade,
> With steps that trod as heavy, yet
> unheard;
> His garments only a slight murmur
> made...
> 'Don Juan', Lord Byron, 1819

*Samuel Taylor
Coleridge*

The Rime of the Ancient Mariner
Ghostly albatross and deliverance

The famous poem published in 1798 by Samuel Coleridge has a dream-like quality to it. Yet, as with all primal dreams, it seems to give us precious signs of the universal values of life.

Three men are on their way to a wedding reception when an old sailor stops them and begs to tell his tale. A ship sails on a fair wind southwards through the Atlantic Ocean. A great storm blows up pulling the ship through mist and snow as far as the Antarctic. Everywhere the crew look they see ice. One day there appears out of the fog a huge bird, an albatross, that seems to be a good omen, for the ice cracks and the ship is blown free. The albatross follows the vessel, perching on mast and rope. But it eats the crew's food and becomes a nuisance.

In a single act of grave import, the mariner shoots the bird dead with his crossbow.

Although at first the crew condemn this as cruel, when the sun shines and a fair wind blows all seems well and they side with the perpetrator. But when the sea is becalmed and the sun blazes hot, all is not so well. Each man weakens with thirst and fatigue. By day they behold slimy creatures crawling over the still sea, by night sparks fly atop the mast (the phenomenon of St Elmo's Fire). It seems a curse has befallen the crew and they hang the dead albatross round the hapless mariner's neck. At last he sees a sign in the distance:

*At first it seemed a little speck,
And then it seemed a mist;
It moved and moved, and took at last
A certain shape, I wist.*

A speck, a mist, a shape,
I wist! And still it neared and neared:
As if it dodged a water-sprite,
It plunged and tacked and veered.

The men recognise the shape of a ship. They are encouraged. But what kind of ship moves without a wind? As the sun sets, the vessel appears as a ghostly 'skeleton of a ship' with only two crew members. One is a spectre woman – 'Life-in-Death' – with red lips, yellow hair, and white skin. The other is her mate, 'Death'. They roll dice for the souls of the crewmen, and Death wins everyone except the ancient mariner. He is the prize of Life-in-Death. So the entire crew die, leaving the mariner alone on the stranded ship. But in time the dead men take on a ghostly form, rising to work the ship:

The loud wind never reached the ship,
Yet now the ship moved on!
Beneath the lightning and the moon
The dead men gave a groan.

They groaned, they stirred, they all uprose,
Nor spake, nor moved their eyes;
It had been strange, even in a dream,
To have seen those dead men rise.

The helmsman steered, the ship moved on;
Yet never a breeze up blew;
The mariners all 'gan work the ropes,
Where they were wont to do;
They raised their limbs like lifeless tools—
We were a ghastly crew.

The body of my brother's son
Stood by me, knee to knee:
The body and I pulled at one rope,

Gustave Dore Ancient Mariner Illustration

But he said nought to me.

Yet these ghostly men are nothing to be feared:

Twas not those souls that fled in pain,
Which to their corses came again,
But a troop of spirits blest:

For when it dawned—they dropped their arms,
And clustered round the mast;
Sweet sounds rose slowly through their mouths,
And from their bodies passed.

So at dawn the ghostly men have loosed the ship to sail on its own, as though driven by the spirit – indeed so fast the mariner falls into a trance. When he comes to he makes out land, identifies lighthouse, hill and church – they are his home land.

In a final twist the phantom ship, perhaps now its duty done, sinks from beneath him and the mariner flounders in the sea. A hermit rescues him and delivers him ashore for the much-awaited wedding. Yet a vesper bell calls him to prayer, which, with a changed heart he observes, instead of attending the wedding. As a result of this strange odyssey the mariner is now a 'sadder but wiser' man: a ghost story with a message.

ST ELMO'S FIRE

For centuries sailors have reported what they regard as ghost lights appearing on their ships. Known as St Elmo's Fire, after the patron saint of Mediterranean sailors, the lights have a bright bluish glow and typically appear as fire at mastheads, or 'lightning', as observed in 'The Rime of the Ancient Mariner'. Jets of fire accompanied by cracking sounds occur during thunderstorms.

Elmo's Fire

Benjamin Franklin

Superstition says that if one of the lights falls to the deck near a crewman he is doomed. But St Elmo's Fire is a good omen. The saint died during a storm at sea but before his death he promised his fellow sailors that if they were not destined to die he would send them a message of salvation. So when sailors see the 'Fire' they believe it is a message from St Elmo that the worst of the storm is passing and that they will survive. A natural explanation for the phenomenon was offered by the physicist Benjamin Franklin in 1749. He claimed the lights are in fact electric: when a storm clears, electricity is discharged through the air and lights appear.

The Browning Circle
English poets fall out

A 19th century medium, Daniel Home, ran a number of séances designed to recruit members to the popular new Spiritualist movement. The poets Robert and Elizabeth Browning were invited to take part in one such meeting arranged in 1855 for an affluent couple who wished to make contact with their son who had tragically died a few years earlier. At the occasion, various 'spiritual' effects were witnessed: table tilting, ghostly hands and knocking. The Brownings had mixed reactions. Elizabeth was bowled over by the experience,

Robert Browning

Robert, on the other hand, thought the whole business an elaborate hoax. The mere fact that his wife was patently seduced by what Robert believed was a construct of tubes and pulleys concealed beneath loose clothing added to his chagrin. Indeed, Robert developed a strong enmity towards Home, who was lampooned mercilessly in *Punch* magazine, and distilled his feelings in a poem, 'Mr Sludge, the Medium.'

Wail of the Banshee
Spectre of family omen

WB Yates was an expert on Irish folklore and had much to say about a certain type of fairy known as the banshee. In both Irish and Scottish traditions, she is believed to attach herself to families. Her appearance is normally regarded as a death omen. Yates states:

Many have seen her as she goes wailing and clapping her hands. The 'keen', the funeral cry of the peasantry, is said to be an imitation of her cry. When more than one banshee is present, and they wail and sing in chorus, it is for the death of some

holy or great one.
    A Treasury of Irish Myth,
    Legend and Folklore, ed. WB Yates.

The banshee is thought to be the ghost of a young woman who has died in childbirth. Her presence fills witnesses with dread as she appears only when a death is imminent in the family. But just how she appears varies with different folkloric traditions. A common form is as a beautiful young woman with long flowing hair, wearing a grey cloak over a red, green or white dress. Alternatively the banshee might be a much more menacing figure who is ugly, because of her buck teeth and single nostril, and has webbed feet and large pendulous breasts. She might be seen washing blood-stained clothes in a stream. Either way, her presence signifies impending death.

Yates also tells of her appearance in other circumstances:

An omen that sometimes accompanies the banshee is the coach-a-bower – an immense black coach, mounted by a coffin, and drawn by headless horses driven by a Dullahan [headless spirit]. It will go rumbling to your door, and if you open it a basin of blood will be thrown in your face. These headless phantoms are found elsewhere than in Ireland.

The myth was transported to America with Irish and Scottish immigrants and has been adapted. One popular version has the banshee haunting the River Tar in Edgcombe, North Carolina. A cohort of British soldiers are terrified to death by the banshee at their riverside camp during the American War of Independence after they had murdered a British mill owner for supporting the rebels.

GHOST HUNTING

Rationalising the Unknown
Psychic societies

With so many reports of sightings of ghosts in the 19th century, in particular, it was not surprising that there was a move to endeavour to 'nail' some as definite

Sigmund Freud

proof of their existence. After all, most were individual experiences which could not be assessed in an objective study. At the same time some less scrupulous members of society saw an opportunity to make money from the gullible and emotionally fragile. A pressing need arose to distinguish between the fake and the serious encounter which led to the founding of two important societies in particular. In 1882 the Society for Psychical Research (SPR) was formed in London dedicated to the examination of spirit activity. As well as investigating instances of ghosts and poltergeist activity, it assessed paranormal faculties, such as Extrasensory Perception (ESP) and hypnosis. The founding fathers from Cambridge University, Sidgewick, Myers and Gurney, were followed by chemist Sir William Crookes, novelist Sir Arthur Conan Doyle, and the psychologists Sigmund Freud and Carl Jung. In the US, a counterpart to the SPR was established in the American Society for Psychical Research (ASPR), whose members tended to come from spiritualist backgrounds rather than the more academic colour of the SPR.

Early Ghost Hunter
Harry Price

One of the more enthusiastic members of the SPR in the first half of the 20th century, and determined to make a breakthrough, was Harry Price. He was the first investigator to use modern technology, such as it was in the 1930s. Before he applied his more scientific tools, investigators relied on eye-witness accounts, photographs and observational integrity. Price's most famous case was Borley Rectory in Essex (see p.21), which he alleged to be 'The Most Haunted House in England', title of the book he later published on the subject.

Having invited himself to this gloomy Victorian pile in 1929, he set up a laboratory there to monitor paranormal events. Instruments included a telescope, portable phone, cameras, sound-deadening felt overshoes, steel tape measure, battery-operated torch, finger-printing equipment, and electro-magnetic lighting. Documenting movements, noises, apparitions on and off for nine years under different incumbents, Price eventually leased the property himself and employed some 40 assistants on the project. However, Price was later discredited as a likely hoaxer – one of the inhabitants of the Rectory, Mrs Smith, later signed a sworn statement that nothing unusual happened at the house until Price arrived.

After his death in 1948 ghost hunting languished for a time. Enthusiasm picked up with the availability of video and audio recording equipment in the 1970s. However, the results of such high-tech investigating have been disappointing, and have tended, if anything, to expose the natural causes that so often lay behind claims to paranormal activity.

Spirit Photography
Catching the ghost

When William Mumler of Boston developed some glass-plate photographs in 1862 he discovered something amazing, or what he took at first sight to be amazing. There behind the main image of the picture were partly transparent faces. He thought he had captured ghosts on film. Although he later realised these were merely double exposures, Mumler also discovered a new source of business: spirit photography. For how better to demonstrate the existence of ghosts, especially spirits of the beloved departed, than to provide a visual record of such phenomenon. A new art quickly flourished on both sides of the Atlantic in producing

Mumler's 'spirit' of Lincoln

photos typically of seated subjects, over whom hovered 'extras' amid a ghostly mist for good effect. Hoaxers everywhere used such techniques with discreetly placed cotton wool to dupe the gullible. However when the public gradually came to learn of the tricks cameras could play the method died away.

Today the camera has become an important tool in the more

sophisticated equipment employed by genuine ghost hunters. Digital cameras are regarded as suspect because computers can so easily manipulate images. Regular 35mm cameras, sometimes fitted with heat-sensitive infrared film, can be set up in places thought to be haunted, ready to be triggered by a sudden change of conditions. Elements associated with ghostly phenomena that might show up on film are streaks of light and mist. Sometimes shapes can be discerned, and orbs of light, invisible to the naked eye, are known to be revealed on film too.

One of the most famous photographs ever taken of a ghost is that of the Brown Lady of Raynham Hall (see p.31) descending a broad staircase. To date no one has been able to offer a plausible explanation.

Since the development of the theory of psychokinesis – by which an individual moves objects or influences mechanical systems by the power of the mind alone – it has been postulated that photographers possessing such powers have projected images on to their film while taking pictures. This process is known as

William Hope Hoax

'thoughtography', a term coined by Tomokichi Fukurai, president of the Psychical Institute of Japan. It has been suggested that intense and determined ghost hunters may be able to spontaneously create imprints on their photographs by such means. However, in the case of the Raynham Hall picture only the photographer's assistant, not the man holding the camera, saw the spirit. The idea of capturing 'spirit energy' on film is still open to abuse by hoaxers but there are said to be a good many examples of inexplicable phenomena caught on film to maintain interest in the camera as an essential tool in the ghost hunter's bag.

Tools of the Trade
The modern ghost hunter's kit

Equipment used in scientific investigations of paranormal phenomena has become a lot more sophisticated since the days of Harry Price. Teams embarking on a serious exploration of premises believed to be haunted will avail themselves of a range of technological instruments.

One tool considered indispensible today is an EMF (Electro Magnetic Field) meter used to measure fluctuations in electromagnetic fields within surroundings. Orthodox science says that such variations are natural. Paranormal researchers believe they can be caused by ghosts in the vicinity. As domestic appliances, such as fridges, microwaves, computers, TVs, can generate EMF, investigators have to

EMF meter ✷

carry out preliminary readings within different zones of the premises to find out what the typical levels are. Then once filming is underway, any anomalous readings can be noted. However, EMF may also arise from natural sources. Thunderstorms produce electric fields in the atmosphere, evidenced by lightning. Certain geological conditions, such as water flowing against rock strata, can heighten an electromagnetic field.

Most investigators will carry both a still camera and a video camcorder. The constant surveillance afforded by the latter is invaluable as it can catch the merest glimpse of ghostly phenomena which would otherwise be missed. It is usually fitted with an infra-red device to visualize in the dark. Other night-vision equipment used would be a light amplification system capable of amplifying light in very gloomy conditions.

A team consisting of several operatives needs to link telephonically and with making as little sound as possible. Headset communicators are therefore a useful accessory and unlike walky-talkies free up the hands allowing them to take notes or man equipment at the same time. Some investigators will take a Geiger counter on site in order to track any changes in ionising radiation levels in the air and surrounding an object. Allied to this is the negative ion counter, which measures the quantity of, and therefore any alteration in, the negative ions in the air. An increase in the volume of negative ions has been linked to paranormal activity.

SIGNS OF THE PHANTOM

With all the monitoring equipment in the world, one may equally be convinced that a place is haunted simply by what is perceived at the time through the natural senses. Apparitions, mists, streaks of light, orbs, strange shadows and their movement may all be symptoms, perhaps only glimpsed for a moment. Sounds such as footsteps, sometimes loud and demonstrative, rapping noises, slamming of doors; even whispered voices, especially of

personages from the past believed to be trapped in some sense – all these sounds might indicate a possible haunting. Some believe smells can be associated with ghosts – scent, tobacco, or an unpleasant stench of disease or dungeon might indicate certain features connected with particular phantoms of the past. Some places suddenly feel unaccountably cold – known as 'cold spots' – because, it is said, spirits may be absorbing heat energy. The converse might also be true, that 'hot spots' indicate a ghost's release of energy into the air. There have indeed been reports of people feeling they have been touched by a ghost: the feeling of being tapped on the shoulder or the brush of clothing against the leg.

The measurements and recordings taken during an investigation are pooled and considered collectively. Any one abnormal reading on its own would not amount to much, but a number of abnormal readings and curious recordings taken together might present a significant picture. There are officially 10,000 haunted sites in Britain alone, though paranormal investigators tend to limit themselves to the most compelling of recent occurrences. Of these, the majority will show no haunting whatsoever, whether because there is no longer any ghostly presence or because there never was any in the first place. So the ghost hunter's task is a painstaking one with a low chance of success.

Charlton House Hunt
Modern day poltergeist

The present library at Greenwich was once a private mansion, Charlton House, owned by William Langhorne, a wealthy East India merchant of the 18th century. It seems that he became so desperate to have a son and heir to his fortune that at the age of 85 he married a 17 year-old maiden. Alas, two months later he was dead. It is said that his restless ghost haunts the building still, especially in rooms on the third floor. There are many grand houses in Britain that are reputed to be haunted but this one is exceptional. Indeed its record is so good that several psychical research societies have investigated and indeed have reported strange phenomena. Inexplicable

Charlton House London

sounds of explosions, cold spots, the unaccountable movements of objects, and strange voices have all been noted. The evidence was so compelling that the BBC decided to include it in a programme about the paranormal broadcast in 1995.

When the library was closed the normal procedure was conducted of searching the rooms to be investigated by the BBC team, together with psychical researcher, Maurice Grosse, famous for the Enfield Poltergeist case. When everyone was satisfied that all was in order, the lights were turned off and the vigil began. At 11pm the sound of an explosion split the air. It came from that room. Turning on the lights, there on the floor in the centre of the room was a blue and white teacup, shattered into seven pieces 'laid' neatly in a circle, as though they had been arranged. The style of the cup was unknown to Charlton House; the explosion was recorded on tape; and no indication of a hoax was ever found.

As you might imagine, further vigils have taken place here – and continue to this day. One similarly extraordinary event happened in July 1999. Members of the Ghost Club conducted a vigil and once again an 'explosion' was heard. This time a test object – a carved wooden mushroom – which had been placed on the floor, had suddenly shot through the air about 3 metres distance. Again no explanation could be found.

The Hex Nightclub
Para. Science investigates

In 2005 a psychical research group, Para.Science, were contacted by the owners of the Hex Nightclub on Merseyside, England, after strange reports from builders who were renovating the place suggested it may be haunted. Eye witnesses told of apparitions in the bar area, in particular of a man dressed in 1940s style clothing, and of dark shapes shifting about. Objects were also reported to move of their own accord. In addition, a phenomenon that caused alarm was the opening of a secure fire door, captured on CCTV, without any apparent agency.

Audible phenomena included the clatter of kitchen utensils and crockery, and inexplicable voices.

An apparition in the basement took the form of a little girl who quickly appeared and disappeared before a member of security.

The day before the CCTV footage of the fire door incident was recorded, a séance was held in the club during which a warning was revealed that a fire would break out at the premises. Several months later, sure enough a fire nearly destroyed the place. The police suspected arson, though there was no apparent motive for such action.

With this somewhat chequered background, the investigation went ahead. It should be pointed out that the building was first erected in the 1860s as a United Presbyterian Chapel. Now it is a venue for Gothic Rock designed on a distinctly satanic theme.

Preliminary tests were carried out to establish a 'baseline' of information about conditions within the club. Floor plans and question sheets were drafted so that any crucial information could be pinpointed. Recording equipment was installed. The main area of interest was the dance room where some apparitions

were reported and the fire door opened. Readings of EMF and temperatures were taken every ten minutes to monitor any fluctuations. At one point before their overnight vigil had begun the lead investigator, Dr Ciarán O'Keeffe, said, 'I'm not easily scared but it is creepy here. We've just noticed that the fire door [kept shut] with the chair has moved. That is hard to explain naturally. Yvette has seen a light anomaly. Steve also recorded it on his digital.'

[*Ghost Hunters, A Guide to Investigating the Paranormal*, by Yvette Fielding and Ciarán O'Keeffe].

The team were certain that before meeting on the dance floor, they had shut and locked all the doors. As an additional precaution, though quite why a locked door should not be considered sufficiently secure is not explained in their report, the team pushed a heavy chair against the fire door. They said, 'You'd need to be very strong to dislodge it [the chair].' At the time when the door must have opened the team were busy preparing their equipment. But the room is not particularly large and they feel that someone would have heard or seen the door open if someone had tried. How it happened remains a mystery.

After patrolling the basement, which proved an unsettling experience with 'a strong smell of horses' that suddenly disappeared and the distinct feeling that the investigators 'aren't alone down here', they returned to the dance room at 11.45pm. They decided to conduct a séance, in the hope of obtaining similarly interesting results to those experienced by the club staff.

Séance

Participants in the séance included the investigating team's co-director, Yvette Fielding, colleague Ann, and three members of staff, one of whom claimed to be psychic. Ciarán and Steve manned the monitoring equipment, as much to check for fraudulent activity as to capture genuine ghost phenomena. An improvised Ouija board was set up using a table with letters and numbers written on it. Each member of the group placed a finger on the rim of a glass at the centre of the table. Yvette led the session by first asking everyone to imagine a guardian light

passing above and below them, then along their arms, slowly circling the group in a clockwise direction to represent energy flowing round.

She called out to invite astral spirits to contact them. The glass started to move but delivered a confused message. Yvette became discouraged but Ciarán urged her to continue because he was noticing erratic readings on a thermal imaging camera. This gadget enabled the user to see precisely what was causing the temperature change, its size and shape. On this occasion Ciarán observed that each time Yvette called out, the monitor showed a 'green fog', indicating a significant drop in temperature about the séance group. Other members of the team checked thermometers in the building and weather reports to ensure there had been no sudden alterations elsewhere.

The séance continued for the time being, and it was worthwhile too. Soon after they resumed, the glass spelled a name, Derek Higgins. He was 45 and wished to confess arson of the building. Further confusion followed and the group abandoned the glass divination but they remained at the table putting their hands together, one on top of another. The psychic member of the group said she sensed a little girl, called Elizabeth, and that she was upset and wished to be comforted. There was no other message and the séance came to an end.

Para.Science were pleased with their findings. Although the team admitted they could not rule out a natural explanation, they feel there was now a good database with which to conduct further investigations of this rather spooky site on Merseyside.

Prominent Investigative Groups and Societies
Roles and aims

The purpose of the Society for Psychical Research is to further the understanding of events and the capabilities of individuals described as 'psychic' or 'paranormal', without prejudice and in a scientific manner.

The Parapsychological Association is an international organisation of scientists and scholars involved in research on psychic experiences, such as telepathy, psychokinesis and clairvoyance, with a view to advancing scientific understanding of these experiences.

The International Survivalist Society is an independent organisation that works with established psychical researchers and parapsychologists throughout the world. It publishes books, articles and photographs on a non-profit basis.

The Survival Research Network is committed to providing scientific assessments of reported phenomena that indicate the survival of human consciousness beyond bodily death.

Para.Science, or Paranormal Science, to give it its full name, researches and investigates all forms of paranormal phenomena. The group is based in the north of England and employs the most advanced techniques available in its studies. All results are available for public scrutiny.

The Parapsychologist aims to disseminate information about paranormal events, and in so doing present a balanced portrayal of the various cases.

INDEX

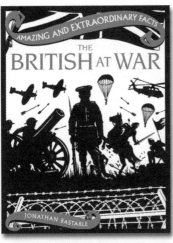

Amazing and Extraordinary
Facts Series: The British At War
Jonathan Bastable
ISBN: 978-1 -910821-237

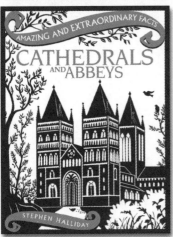

Amazing and Extraordinary
Facts Series: Cathedrals &
Abbeys
Stephen Halliday
ISBN: 978-1 -910821-046

For more great books visit our website at **www.rydonpublishing.co.uk**

Picture credits

p6 Ian Robinson
p62 Merry Barrentine, Utah Paranormal Exploration and Research
p71 David Corby Miskatonic,
p109 Turquoisefish